In and Out of the Working Class

In and Out of the
Working
Class

Michael D. Yates

ARBEITER RING PUBLISHING · WINNIPEG

Copyright © 2009 Michael D. Yates

Arbeiter Ring Publishing
201E-121 Osborne Street
Winnipeg, Manitoba
Canada R3L 1Y4
www.arbeiterring.com

Printed in Canada by Transcontinental Printing
Cover by Branden Douglas
Typeset by Relish Design Studio, Ltd.

 MANITOBA ARTS COUNCIL
CONSEIL DES ARTS DU MANITOBA
YEARS/ANS

 Canada Council   Conseil des Arts
for the Arts   du Canada

 Canadian   Patrimoine
Heritage   canadien

With assistance of the Manitoba Arts Council/Conseil des Arts du Manitoba.

We acknowledge the support of the Canada Council for our publishing program.

ARP acknowledges the financial support to our publishing activities of the Manitoba
Arts Council/Conseil des Arts du Manitoba, Manitoba Culture, Heritage and
Tourism, and the Government of Canada through the Book Publishing Industry
Development Program (BPIDP).

Printed on 100% post-consumer-waste recycled paper.

Library and Archives Canada Cataloguing in Publication

Yates, Michael, 1946-
    In and out of the working class/Michael D. Yates.

ISBN 978-1-894037-35-8

    1. Yates, Michael, 1946-. 2. Working class—United States—Social
conditions. 3. Equality—United States. 4. Economists—United States—
Biography. I. Title.

HD8073.Y38A3 2009   330.092   C2008-906937-4

DEDICATION

To Karen Korenoski, who, through good times and bad,
has been my constant companion.

I.
Growing Up Working Class

The Year of the Strike

FICTION

With a slight shrug of his shoulders, he began to move toward the line. He took four steps, the last one ending in a slide, and as he did so he swung the ball, first forward and then backward in a razor-straight arc until it reached its peak cupped in his large hands about halfway between his waist and his shoulders. On the third step, his arm swung forward, again in that pure arc, and he released the ball just after his swing reached its lowest point. As he imparted just the right lift and spin with his fingers, the ball hit the lane almost silently, as if it had never touched down at all, the bowling equivalent of the dribbling of Earl Monroe, who was able to make it appear as if the basketball never left his hand as he snaked through and around his defenders toward the hoop. The ball slid effortlessly toward its destination sixty feet away, gripped the wood where the oil ended and, now rotating and spinning, drove relentlessly high into the one-three pocket, pushing the pins straight back into the pit. As he stood motionless, his left leg bent and his right hand stretched out and upward toward the second arrow target, Jimmy Beck grinned, watching his artistry unfold. Around him, the other bowlers, with their nicknames — Sky, Smoky, Moe, Pooch, Beaver, Butch — sewn above the pockets of their team shirts, stopped to watch perfection.

It was right around the time that Jimmy was first beginning to tear up the lanes that I hit upon my money-making plan. November of 1958. The year of the big strike.

I was sixteen and a high school senior. I hated school. Teachers kept telling me that I was smart and had a lot of potential. I just didn't apply myself. If I did, I could go to college and, though it was never said, get out of this one-stoplight, factory town. But I was skeptical. I often hear people talk about a teacher who inspired them. None of my teachers inspired me. I thought then that they were a sorry lot. I liked a couple of them. One science teacher was a kindly old man, although his breath stunk. It was said that he had been in the Bataan death march. He certainly looked the part, all thin and gaunt with bad teeth and a pained expression engraved permanently on his face. The social studies teacher, a phlegmatic old woman who moved at such a slow pace that she was nicknamed "Turtle," tried mightily to interest us in things like the Indian caste system. Sometimes I'd listen, but mostly I would stare out the window at that one stoplight as it slowly changed from red to green to yellow, over and over again. All I could do was to hope the bell would ring soon.

When I wasn't gazing out the window, I filled my notebook with miniature bowling lanes and pool tables. I'd draw a bowling alley, complete with pins and the seven arrows that served as ball targets. Then I would trace out a perfect strike trajectory with my pen, right up high in the one-two pocket, since I was a left-handed bowler. Sometimes I'd admit to an error and leave a pin or two. Then I'd draw a new lane and a new line to pick up the spare. Most fun were the splits, a five-ten or a two-seven baby split, or if I were in an adventurous mood, a tough one like the four-seven-ten. After about ten minutes of working out the proper hooks and trajectories, I'd switch to pool. On my tablet table I would lay out a few balls in random spots. Then I would place the cue ball somewhere in the middle of the table and begin to plot out the shots. I'd figure just where to hit the cue ball, how hard, and with what english. I'd draw a line from the cue ball to the object ball, another line from the object ball to the appropriate pocket, and a third line showing how the cue ball would roll after it hit the object ball. This was a great game because I never missed a shot, and the cue ball always ended up in perfect position for the next one.

I suppose most people would see my little classroom amusements as immature, even pathetic. But in sports and games, the more you visualize what you will do when you are really playing, the more comfortable you will be actually doing it. At home, I studied my form in front of the mirror in my bedroom and practised my delivery endlessly on the linoleum and the hardwood floors. In the cellar, I had a set of plastic pins and balls and was down there at all hours devising new grips and releases, much to the chagrin of my parents. I also bought books to improve my skills. For bowling, I had a book by Buddy Bomar, a professional from Texas against whom my dad had bowled a few games at the Corpus Christi naval base from which he was being mustered out of the service at the end of the war. Dad told me that German prisoners of war set the pins and that the price of a game was three cents. He also bragged that he had beaten Bomar a couple of times, but I wondered about this. For pool, my bible was a little gem by Willie Mosconi, who I found out later made the tough shots in the movie *The Hustler*.

I wanted to do whatever I could to get higher bowling scores and shoot better pool. If you were going to do something, you ought to do it right. You couldn't use a house ball or a pair of shoes you rented from behind the counter; you had to have your own. This was especially true if you were left-handed. House bowling balls were made for right-handers, so the middle two fingers you use for bowling never fit properly if you were a lefty. The soles of house shoes were either too slippery or too sticky. I bought my own ball and shoes soon after my dad and my grandfather first took me to the lanes. Both of them were good bowlers, especially grandpa, who had averaged in the high 190s in the late 1920s, a sensationally high average given the primitive state of bowling technology then. He even had his own radio bowling show, called *The Kingpin.* The kingpin is the five pin, and it stands in the middle of the triangle setup of ten pins. Getting your ball to drive through the pocket and contact the five pin is the key to bowling success. Dad wasn't as good as his father, but I remember reading in his high school yearbook that he "could give even his father a run for his money."

The first ball I owned had a conventional grip, one in which the finger holes were drilled knuckle-deep. The best bowlers were using the fingertip grip, which, as the name implies, has finger holes only deep enough to accommodate the first finger joints. Such a grip allowed you to get more "lift" on the ball, making it hook more effectively into the pocket and more likely to take out the kingpin and make a strike. I lusted after such a ball. I saved money to buy one and got my local alley to get me a discount at the lanes in the next town, where they had ball-drilling facilities. My aunt, herself an accomplished kegler, drove me over, and I had the new ball drilled—a black Manhattan Rubber. The proprietor said I could bowl a game on the house to test the fit. The ball fit like a glove, and that first game I threw a 242.

Pool was different in terms of equipment. You could get an adequate cue at the pool hall, although the sticks on the racks tended to warp and were often too light. Willie Mosconi said to use a heavy cue, at least twenty ounces, and one with a thick tip. Such cues weren't always available, so I went to a supply shop in Pittsburgh, about forty miles away, and got my own two-piece cue, twenty-two ounces, and with a fat tip. My game improved dramatically.

Fantasy and makeshift games are fine, but practice makes perfect. I had to get to the lanes and the pool hall and play as often as possible, especially if I wanted to beat my imaginary scores. But this presented a problem. My parents were strict and wanted to know where I was at all times. And they didn't want me squandering my money. I had been delivering newspapers since I was twelve and, compared to the other carriers, had built a large and lucrative route. I was expected to put nearly all of the money I made in a bank account, to be used to pay for part of my college education, which both of my parents took for granted. The old man had not worked like a dog in the glass factory and my mom had not slaved away at home with four kids to see their oldest child waste his life. Education was the ticket, and there were to be no ifs, ands, or buts about it. This meant that I wasn't to spend my time in pool halls hanging around drunks and derelicts. Bowling was okay in moderation, which meant once a week. Occasionally I was allowed to bowl a game after my father's and my grandpa's league games were done, a reward for my keeping score for the teams. But no more than this.

So I waged a war of deception. Some paper customers gave me tips when I collected their bills once a month. I lied about these and kept the difference. I collected pop bottles and kept the deposit money. Sometimes my grandparents gave me money, and this was added to my stash. Once I had accumulated some money, an additional problem arose. I had to find a place to hide it. My father was always spying, trying to find my money.

For a while, I had a perfect hideaway. My father had been a radioman in the navy during the war, stationed in the South Pacific. After the war, he bought an old Hallicrafters shortwave radio. He gave it to me, and I had it on the desk beside my bed. I loved how the tubes lit up my room when I turned out the night light. I had a long wire antenna strung out the window and connected to the top of a tall pole to which our basketball bank board was connected, about a hundred feet away. This gave me clear AM reception, and at night I listened to all the great stations east of the Mississippi river, such as WOWO in Fort Wayne, WCKY in Cincinnati, WABC in New York City, WBZ in Boston, KYW in Philadelphia, and, the oldest AM station in the country, KDKA in Pittsburgh. I listened to high school, college, and professional basketball games; news from different parts of the country; and rock and roll. The low disembodied voices and the eerie green lights made going to sleep something special. The top of the large radio could be opened easily to get at the tubes, and the ample spaces inside seemed a spy-proof hiding place for my money. It was—for a while.

Now I had to get out of the house to bowl and shoot pool. It wasn't hard to get out of the house. But I couldn't take the bowling ball or the cue stick without my parents knowing my destination. I noticed that neither of them paid any attention to my equipment. I normally kept it in the basement, and, although my mom did the laundry there, she didn't seem to notice the various boxes, tools, and sundry items scattered about. My father seldom went in the cellar, unless he had to get a plumber's snake to clean the sump pump. Since they just assumed that the ball and cue were in the cellar, I began to leave them at the bowling alley and pool hall. The counter person at the lanes let me keep the ball behind the desk so I wouldn't have to rent a locker. Raymie, the guy who ran the pool room, said I could keep my cue in the locked rack at the back of the hall. Now whenever I left the house, I could just hike down the hill to town, sneak off to my two dens of iniquity, and practise. I just had to make sure that I practised at times when none of my dad's buddies were there. And I had to get a friend to give me a lift home to put my gear in its accustomed place on those occasions when I might legitimately ask to go bowling or shoot pool. A couple of times when I went to the lanes with my dad, he asked me why I didn't have my ball with me.

I told him I had forgotten and left it at the bowling alley the last time we went. He never seemed to catch on. He probably had more important things on his mind.

My father worked in the large glass factory that dominated the town, which was named for the founder of the company, a pioneer in the manufacturing of glass. There was a large bronze statue of this man in the town's park. He had run his company as a feudal manor, much like the small mining towns that dotted the landscape along the wide river, which was the source of beautiful white sand used to make the glass. The plant itself was strung out along the river from the bridge at the lower end of town to 13th street, over a mile in all.

Like many industrial serfs, the men and women in the glass factory joined the great CIO union army of the 1930s and brought an end to their serfdom. The big battles were won after the war when the soldiers came home and took to the picket lines. They had seen too much shit in the war to take much of it at home. By the time I was in the first grade, the factory and the town had been transformed by high wages, good benefits, and a grievance procedure.

But if the union had brought prosperity to the masses, it had also made an implacable enemy of the company. Inside the factory there was chronic guerilla warfare as the workers sought to expand the freedoms they had won with their union and the company tried to win back what it had lost. Grandpa, the bowling ace, was also a time-study engineer at the plant. He had mastered the arcane but potent techniques of Frederick Taylor despite having only an eighth-grade education. During the war, he had even taught time-study at a local college. Grandpa was in the front line of the daily factory wars, ever present with his stop watch, trying to uncover ways to make more glass with less labour. Many years later, when my father's lungs were about to give up the ghost, he blurted out from his oxygen tent in the intensive care unit of the local hospital that his dad had even time-studied him once.

Over the long haul, the company waged a war of attrition. Not only did it rely less on union labour by raising efficiency at the plant, but it also opened new plants in places where it would be hard for the union to follow. After the war, new plants were built in rural areas far away from the industrial heartland, especially in the South. Once these plants were up and running, they were used to threaten the union plants; either the union would have to moderate its demands or the union plants would close. In the mid-1950s, the company discovered a new method for mass-producing plate glass. Rumors circulated that the plant in our town would be refitted for the new process, thus guaranteeing that it would stay put for the indefinite future. But in return, the company wanted a rewrite of the collective bargaining agreement, one which would have wiped out most of the work rules the union had fought so hard to secure. When the old agreement expired, the company put forward its radical proposal, complete with a propaganda campaign to frighten the workers and their families. It was common to hear people talking on street corners about the possibility that the factory would close unless the union accepted the company's proposals. The union and the workers, however, stood firm and refused to make concessions. After ten weeks of desultory negotiations, the union called the company's bluff and put the workers on the picket lines—for eight months.

At the time, I didn't know any of this. I knew little about my father's work, and we never learned about such things in school. Other than an occasional complaint about a particular boss or conversations with my mother about his incentive pay, I don't remember him saying much about the plant or what went on there. He certainly didn't tell us about the strike. One day he went to work; the next day he stayed home. Every couple of days, he did his picket duty. I do remember that grandpa stopped coming up to the house. And sad for me, the company-sponsored bowling leagues were suspended.

Most of the factory families lived lives of fixed routines. The husband left home five days a week, and not always at the same time, since he worked shifts. The wife stayed home and took care of the kids and the household. The kids went to school. Dad brought home the money, and though mom might take care of it, you knew to go to your father if you needed some. His earning of the money through hard work at the factory was what gave him his sense of self. The strike disrupted this routine and created peculiar tensions. Extra money had been put aside in anticipation of a strike, but no one expected the strike to drag on month after month. The union had a strike fund, but it didn't come close to making up for missed paychecks. Money was soon in short supply. Mortgage payments, car payments, doctor and dentist bills—all of the mundane outflows of cash that help define a working class life—couldn't be made. There was no spare change for treats, such as candy, movies, pizza, bowling; even birthday presents got short shrift. If the women could have gone to work, they would have, but things weren't set up that way in those days. I began to get an idea of how bad things were when my dad "borrowed" the stash of money I had hidden in the radio.

Money troubles were compounded by the constant presence of dad at home. This messed up our daily regimen. Dad did his regular chores, but these didn't keep him busy enough. There weren't many of mom's chores he could do. He could make popcorn, penuche and sea foam fudge, and eggs, but, except for the eggs, these wouldn't make much of a meal for six people. And if he did the cooking, cleaning, and laundry, what would mom do? You could feel the tensions mounting as the money supply dwindled and they got in each other's way. My mother had grown up poor, and the insecurity now enveloping our household was stripping away her normally calm persona.

My parents seldom argued, at least not in front of us. But I woke up one night to hear them talking in their bedroom, which was below my own. My mom was crying, saying, "What are we going to do?"

My dad said, "Everything will be OK," but the muffled voice I heard didn't sound convincing. They must have gotten up and gone into the kitchen, because I could no longer hear them. When I came downstairs in the morning, my mother told me that dad had gone to my uncle's in Cleveland to help out in his brother's shop there. He'd make some money, and this would ease our financial woes. My uncle was an artist; he sandblasted designs into pieces of glass. He was talented but a lousy businessman. Mom said that dad would help him with deliveries and collections.

With dad away, mom found it hard to contain her anxieties. She perpetually had a worried look on her face, and when she didn't think anyone could hear, she would sigh. Mom's anxiety spread to the rest of us. I had a sick feeling in the pit of my stomach, nothing I could explain if asked — an inchoate fear that something bad was about to happen. I tried to lose myself in daydreams. I fantasized about girls, pool, and bowling, but my mother's troubled face kept intruding.

I remember the exact moment I hit upon my plan. I was drifting off to sleep listening to the radio when I heard one of my favorite songs, "To Know Him Is To Love Him" by the Teddy Bears. I was thinking about a pretty girl I had a crush on when it came to me. If I had a stake, I could win enough money shooting pool and bowling to make my mother smile again. The details of my scheme emerged as I lay in my bed, and I fell asleep as Tommy Edwards crooned "Please Love Me Forever."

I seldom went into my parents' bedroom. Although I never thought of them as having lives independent of mine, some subconscious part of me told me that they did and that it was centred in this room. I entered it with trepidation. My mother was visiting a neighbor, so this was my chance. The room was dark even though it was mid-morning, so I had to turn on the light. I hurried over to the dresser on the opposite side of the room and opened the upper left-hand drawer. This is where my parents kept their envelopes. They had devised a simple scheme to budget their money: they kept an envelope for each spending category. There was an envelope for "house payment," one for "gas bill," one for "electric," one for "groceries," and so on. Every payday, my father put money in the envelopes, and they used these monies to pay each bill when it came due. After all these weeks of the strike, I guessed that not many envelopes would have money inside. I started rifling through them, and I was beginning to worry that none would contain any cash. But the one marked "house payment" did—$50. I took the money, put it in my pocket, and quickly left the room.

I fussed and fidgeted until my mother came back. As soon as she got in the door, I told her that I had called my friend Sam and he had invited me to come over to his house. I said he had also told me that I could stay for supper and then watch television. She said fine but not to be home too late. I asked her if I could come home by midnight, and she said all right. Sam lived a short distance away, so I could just walk. I had another cup of coffee, grabbed some cookies, put on my heavy coat, and left.

I knew that, barring an emergency, my mother would never call Sam's house, so I wasn't worried about my lie. When you're a teenager, lying to your parents becomes second nature, probably a part of your attempt to break free from them and become your own person. I nonchalantly walked down our street toward Sam's, but when I got out of sight of our house, I turned toward the highway and the path down the steep hill toward town. The path was slippery from the recent snow, and I had to be careful not to slip and have to explain why my clothes were muddy. At one particularly treacherous turn, I chuckled as I remembered how we had pushed one of the snotty little Smolek brothers over the edge the week before on our way to school. His mother had come screaming to our door, but I denied everything and, for a change, my mother believed me. Probably because she couldn't stand Mrs. Smolek.

It took me about twenty-five minutes to get to the pool hall. I got my cue from the wall rack and began to practise on the back table. Raymie was cutting hair and selling numbers to a steady stream of customers. Saturday was always a busy day for both activities. Men becoming desperate from the strike gave Raymie their quarters and half dollars and prayed for the number they had dreamt about to hit. I paid no attention to any of this. I methodically practised my spot shots, banks, and difficult cuts. I knew right away that I had my stroke.

About one o'clock every Saturday, the three Dawson brothers came to town to play pool. "Here come the hicks from the sticks," we'd say. They were farm boys, big and strong, not too savvy in the ways of the world. Their clothes, their boots, the way they talked, their hand-rolled smokes, everything about them said "hayseed." Friendly and naive, they were unaware that they were the butt of our jokes. Of course, we were never too obvious, because they were tough fellows.

The brothers entered the poolroom right on schedule. They exchanged a few corny jokes with Raymie and some of the customers who knew them. Just as I had hoped, all of the tables were taken when they arrived. They looked around disappointed and sat down on three of the high chairs spectators used to watch the action when the good players were shooting. After about ten minutes, I walked over and asked them if they wanted to play. They said, "Sure."

The Dawson brothers always had money, and they liked to gamble. After a couple of dull games of rotation, the oldest brother, Roy, asked me if I wanted to play "points." This was a game of rotation pool in which the five, ten, and fifteen balls were "point" balls, worth whatever amount of money you were playing for. Whichever player pocketed the highest number of balls during the game also got a point. The minimum number of "points" in a game was four. However, it was possible for there to be more than four points in a game. In rotation pool, the shooter has to strike the lowest numbered ball on the table with the cue ball. Once the lowest numbered ball is struck, any balls that are pocketed count for the shooter. So, if you hit the one ball into a "point" ball and the "point ball" went into a pocket, the "point ball" counted for you. The same was true if you made a point ball on the break (assuming you hit the one ball first) or by caroming the cue ball off the object ball and into a "point ball." If a player made a "point ball" out of sequence as a result of a combination, carom, or break shot, this counted as a point, but the point ball was re-spotted to be shot in its proper rotation. It was possible, therefore, that there would be six or seven points a game, or more, so you could win a lot of money in a game. Each player had to pay the others the difference between the value of his points and that of each other player.

To let me know that they weren't pikers, Roy asked if fifty cents a point would be all right. This was a pretty high stake for me, but I said, "OK." We played "points" for nearly two hours. The two younger brothers made a few lucky shots, enough to keep them in the game, but eventually Roy and I won their money.

Roy was a goofy-looking character, with out-of-style glasses, greasy slicked-back black hair, and Dickey jeans rolled up at the cuffs. A big-buckled belt, white socks, and worn imitation cordovan dress shoes completed the outfit. He chewed on a cheap DeNobili cigar, which made him look particularly ridiculous, but at least he never lit it. His oddball character carried over to his pool playing. He gripped his cue between his first two fingers, with his thumb up in the air. It was a disarming style, because opponents figured he couldn't possibly make shots like that. But he could and did. When his brothers dropped out of the game, I could tell he was gaining confidence that he could beat me. He began to chatter and cackle and almost swallowed his cigar when he knocked the cue ball around three rails to pocket a point ball. His brothers cheered and started to make snide remarks about my talent.

I was still a few dollars ahead when two guys I knew asked if they could shoot. Unless two of the better players were shooting for high stakes, it wasn't acceptable to deny new entrants into a game. Roy thought he was on a roll, so he didn't care. The new players, "Hack" and "Pep" were good players, and I wasn't keen on their playing, but I didn't have a choice. Fortunately, Roy's luck deserted him while mine went wild. We had upped the ante to a dollar a point, and in the first game, I made an incredible six points to none for my three opponents. I made a point ball on the break, and over the course of the game, I made all three point balls in their turn, made a combination shot that put in a point ball, and pocketed the largest number of balls. Eighteen dollars in one game. An hour later, I walked out of the poolroom with about $100 in winnings. Roy and his brothers put on their coats and glumly followed me out. Hack and Pep were complaining that I didn't give them a chance to get their money back. I ignored them and laughed to myself. My day had begun auspiciously.

Next to the poolroom was a seedy bar, a hangout for alcoholics and the boarders who lived upstairs. All day long the bartender and his wife kept hot sausages and sliced onions cooking on a small grill behind the bar. For twenty-five cents you could buy a sausage sandwich served on a hard roll. I bought two, as well as a Coke, went over to a booth, and gorged myself. Five minutes later, I headed for the bowling alley a few blocks away.

It was just before seven o'clock when I got to the lanes at the Slovak Catholic Union club, "CU" for short. I took my ball from behind the counter, got a lane, put on my shoes, and began to practice. There wasn't much league action on Saturday night, so most of the lanes were free. I loosened up with a few practise balls, and then kept score. I bowled two games: 223 and 217. By the end of the second game, I was locked in, every ball driving into the one-two pocket. I was ready.

The good bowlers began to drift in around eight o'clock. A couple of guys practised, but most of the men stood and talked. There wasn't much of the sarcastic banter you usually heard and hardly any laughter. Every Saturday night, the town's best bowlers competed for money. It was called "pot bowling." Before the strike, games went on long into the night and hundreds of dollars changed hands. The games continued during the strike, but the pots were smaller. And the bowling got more desperate because the men needed the money for rent and food.

Pot bowling was uncomplicated. Each man put money into the pot. Then the men were put into pairs by lot, drawing numbered pills out of a container. One and two were paired, three and four, and so forth, until each bowler was paired. The pot was split between the bowler who got the highest score and the pair whose combined score was the highest; the high scorer received one-half of the pot and the high pair got one-half to divide between them. The pairs would change every game, as would the pair of alleys you bowled on. Usually, four to six players bowled on one pair of lanes. How many lanes were used depended on the number of participants in the pot.

I spotted a bowler I knew and asked him if I could bowl. He said that anyone with money could join but I might have to wait if there was not an even number of bowlers. The men were beginning to put their balls on the ball return, so I took mine and placed it with the others. We began to bowl "shadow balls," practice shots thrown with no pins set up at the end of the lanes. I counted twelve bowlers, a perfect number — six pairs on two sets of lanes. As if on cue, Jimmy Beck shook the box of pills, and the first set of pairs were formed. I drew a good bowler with the odd nickname of "Shanghai." I was hoping for Jimmy Beck, but so was everyone else.

As soon as the men noticed that a teenager was bowling, they began to badger me.

"Sure you got enough money kid."

"Hope you don't cry when you lose your dough."

"Hey, isn't your old man making enough money out there in Cleveland?" This last jibe was made by a big guy nicknamed "Butch," a person neither I nor my father liked. I was about to say something, but an older man who bowled with my grandpa, and who had recently hit the phenomenal three-game score of 803, said to me in a quiet voice, "Don't let Butch bother you. The union gave your dad permission to go to Cleveland, and he isn't getting his strike benefits either."

"Fuck you, Butch," I said under my breath as I grabbed my ball and took my practise shots.

I bowled well, but not well enough. We were playing for $20 a game. I started with $140, and after five games I was down to $40. If my partners' scores had been as high as mine, I would have at least shared a couple of pots, but it seemed that no matter who my mates were, they bowled better with another partner. In the second game, I made seven strikes in a row and bowled a 258, but Jimmy Beck struck out in his last frame and made a 259. My partner scored a 180; Jimmy's bowled a 221.

I thought about quitting. I could put $40 back in the envelope, and maybe my parents would think that was all they had put in it. But I didn't, and when Jimmy announced that a majority had agreed to raise the pot to $30, I laid down my money. Two bowlers dropped out, and this left ten. There was $300 in the pot, more money than I had ever held in my hand at one time. I promised myself that if I won any money I would quit and go home. A win would mean at least $75; if I got high game and high pair, I'd pocket $225. If I lost, I'd have to go home anyway.

I took my pill and called out my number—eight. I would be paired with whoever drew the seven. Since Jimmy Beck held the pill box, he got the last pill. I listened as the numbers were called out—two, six, ten. I said a prayer, "Let Jimmy be the seven." One, three, nine, four, and...five! Jimmy was the seven. I had a chance.

Jimmy and I were on the right-hand set of lanes, along with four other bowlers. The other four players were on the left-hand pair of alleys. I liked the right pair better than the left, so I was even more confident that I would win some money.

For the next few minutes, I was in a kind of trance. I visualized in my mind what I was going to do, just like I did in my history class. And then I did it. I was the first bowler, and I bowled first on the left lane of the pair and then on the right, in succession. When the sixth bowler finished on the left lane, I started over again.

Bowlers are always fussing to make their fingers feel comfortable in the ball. Pressure makes hands moist and slippery. Fingers swell and shrink. So they use resin to keep their hands dry, and they keep tape and scissors in their bags so that they can put tape in or remove tape from the holes. Collodion was put on the blisters that often afflicted the inside of a bowler's thumb. Amazingly, my hands were unusually dry, and my grip was firm and comfortable. I began with a strike, converted a one-pin spare, and then threw four successive strikes, each ball setting in the oil and hitting perfectly on target in the one-two pocket. Jimmy matched me strike for strike. We were way ahead of the two other teams on our lanes. I checked the bowlers on the other pair. The score sheets were made of clear plastic and set in a special holder under a bright light which reflected the scores onto a screen above the lanes. I noticed with alarm that "Sky," the man who had scored the 803, was on a six-bagger—six strikes in a row. His partner had three spares and a triple. They were more than thirty pins ahead of us, and Sky was twenty pins ahead of both me and Jimmy.

I stopped watching our rivals' scores and concentrated on my own, but I knew that this contest would go down to the last frame. I struck again and so did Jimmy. A collective groan arose at the other table, and I saw that Sky had thrown a difficult split. When he missed, I thought we were home free. But we weren't, and as I stepped up to bowl my last frame, I knew that this frame would determine the winners. If I struck out, I would have another 258 and the highest score.

I dried my hand over the fan, picked up my ball, carefully fitted my fingers and thumb into the three holes, took my starting position just to the right of centre, bent into the stooped stance I had copied from my grandpa, and focused my eyes on the second arrow target. I imagined my four steps and slide and then executed them. I felt that it was a good shot right away, and as I watched the ball skid, catch, and hook toward the pocket, I arrogantly turned and walked back to the starting line. I heard the pins crash and peeked around in time to see the last pins tumble into the pit.

I would have bet the money I had saved for college that I would get two more strikes and win at least $150. I repeated the same ritual as I had on the first strike. As I took my second step, I heard Butch say in a voice just loud enough to be heard, "Smart-ass, fucking punk." I should have stopped my delivery and started over. But I didn't and as soon as I released the ball, I knew I had pulled it to the right. It drove straight into the one pin and hit exactly on the nose. Only eight pins fell, leaving the two and four pins. I was so disgusted that I rushed the spare shot and chopped the two pin off the four. My score was 245. I kept my head down as I took a seat.

Sky's partner finished with a 226. Jimmy decided to wait until Sky bowled before he did, so we all turned to watch Sky complete his game. He had 196 in the eighth frame and a spare in the ninth. He needed all three strikes in the tenth frame to beat me. His first two shots were strikes, square in the pocket. Sky had a crooked face and a harelip, so it wasn't easy to read his expressions. But he was grinning as he got ready for his final ball. He threw a wide hook, unusual in that day of hard rubber balls, which didn't naturally curve the way modern balls do. He let the ball go to the right of his usual target, but it came roaring back from the gutter toward the pocket. Then it froze and straightened out just as it hit the pins. This caused the six to fly around the ten and leave the ten pin standing. I rejoiced at the thought of at least a tie for high game, but then the one pin, which had been sent flying to the left, hit the side board at the very end of the lane and came bouncing back onto the lane sliding directly toward the ten pin. The automatic pin-setting machine was in motion, ready to sweep the lane clean and re-rack the pins. "Hurry up," I shouted, but to no avail. The one pin nicked the ten pin and sent it wobbling into the gutter. Sky had a 246. Sky and his partner now had a team total of 472.

I still had hope. Jimmy Beck had 198 in the eighth frame and a spare in the ninth frame. He could bowl a 248. But he only needed a spare and a small count on his final ball for us to have the high team total. I didn't see how we could lose. He hadn't missed a spare all night and had struck almost every time he bowled on the right-hand lane of our pair.

When bowlers throw what looks like a perfect shot and they leave one pin, they say they got "tapped." The most common tap for a right-handed bowler is the ten pin; the tap occurs when the six pin wraps around the ten pin but doesn't touch it. There is usually a good reason for this. The ball may have hit the pocket too "light," that is, not high enough in the one-three pocket. Or it may have hit the pocket at too sharp of an angle. Or a pin may have been "off spot"—not exactly where it should have been as a result of a slight mechanical malfunction by the automatic pin setter. A worse tap, and the only one that bowlers say is a true tap, is the nine pin. Here the ball drives so strongly into the pocket that it hits the kingpin too close to its centre, so close that the ball then drives straight through the five and fails to deflect into the nine. Jimmy's first ball did just this. The crowd gasped in disbelief, and Jimmy shouted out "Shit!" I wasn't upset though. The nine pin was one of the easiest spares to convert. A right-hander just had to stand a little to the left of where he usually began his approach and throw the same ball as for a strike. It was almost impossible to miss. Jimmy confidently grabbed his ball as soon as it rolled up the ball return and almost without hesitation took off down the approach. The ball was thrown off target to the right, but there wasn't much oil near the gutters, so I waited for it to stop skidding and hook into the pin. But it never caught the lane, and about ten feet from the pin it fell ignominiously into the gutter. His score was 226, and our total was 471. I got my ball and took off my shoes and put them in my bag. Sky said, "Tough luck, kid," and approached Jimmy to collect the money. I took my bag to the counter and had the counterman put it underneath. I looked back once and walked out the door.

The path leading up the hill toward home was a few blocks from the club. It had begun to rain, so I walked as fast as I could. Parts of the path were icy, and I almost fell just as I reached the top. I once again crossed the highway. I cut through the rear neighbor's yard and walked around to the front of our house. A light was on in the living room, and I said to myself, "Oh shit. Mom's still awake." But she was dozing on the couch. As I opened the door, she jumped up and said, "I thought you were staying at Sam's 'til midnight."

I had forgotten about this, but I ad-libbed, "He had a big fight with his mom, so I decided to come home early."

"Oh," she said. "Guess what?" she asked. "Your dad called and told me that the strike is over. He said his buddy Nick called and gave him the news. Nick said the company got most of what it wanted, but at least people will be getting paychecks." I was too stunned to talk, but she didn't notice and just said, "Boy, that's good news. I don't know what we would have done if the strike had lasted much longer." Then she added, "I baked a cherry pie if you want a piece." I wasn't hungry, but I shuffled into the kitchen and ate some pie. Mom said, "You'd better get to bed." We said goodnight, and I climbed the stairs to my room. I turned on the radio and turned off the light. My bedroom was always cold in the winter, so I piled on the covers, arranging them so the top sheet was the only thing touching my skin. Alan Freed was DJing on WABC. Conway Twitty began to sing "It's Only Make Believe." If only it were. I usually sang along, but I had to try to figure out how to solve my fifty-dollar problem. The strike might be over, but my troubles were just beginning.

Irene: my Mother

NON-FICTION

It was early in February, and Irene was waiting for the school bus along with the other high school students. They were all poor, the children of Italian immigrants, whose fathers worked in the coal mine down by the river. It was 1941 and the depression still raged, though there was more work now than there had been in a long time. She had come to this town when she was twelve years old, just a few years earlier, after her father, Dante, died. They had lived in another Pennsylvania town, a little bigger than this one and with some jobs available besides mining, but they had moved here to be close to her maternal relatives. Dante's mother had insisted that Irene's mother, Lucia, take care of Dante's brother, but Lucia's mother had forbade this.

It had been a hard few years; they were among the poorest families in what to an outsider must have appeared a uniformly desolate place. There was no regular employment for a woman, so Lucia took in laundry and mended other people's clothes. She and her brother, Dan, helped, struggling to carry water from the pump and heat it on the coal stove. Their house was rented from the coal company, a small place with tarpaper shingles and no indoor plumbing or central heating.

The upstairs bedrooms were freezing cold. Fires were a constant threat, and just the past winter a neighbor's house had burned, killing the family's young daughter. Fifty years later, Irene still got depressed during the winter months remembering that fire.

As Dan laughed with his friends, Irene thought about things. She did not have many friends from the town in which the high school was located. This was a factory village three miles up the river. It was home to an enormous glass factory, one of the biggest in the world, and a large pottery. You could see the great piles of white sand used to make the glass on the other side of the old iron bridge that led into the town. The town itself, although modest in size, had many shops and bars and churches; one of the churches was made of stone and had marble altars and floors. Compared to the mining town, with its wooden church, company store, and tiny post office, the factory town was the big city. Most of the men worked in one of the factories, and their children, especially those whose fathers had better jobs, made up the "in groups" at school. They had nicer clothes, spending money, and old jalopies. They snubbed the poor "dago" mining kids. So did some of the teachers.

Irene felt the condescension and wondered if something was wrong with her. Her friends told her that she was pretty, but she doubted it. How could anyone from her town be pretty? Sometimes she wished she could be more like her brother. He had "the gift of gab" and lots of friends. He was wild and got in trouble, but nobody pushed him around. He was a boy though, and that made all the difference.

She felt more at home in the mining town. There was no shame in being poor here. Everyone was in the same boat and nearly everyone was Italian, so people stuck together and showed each other the small kindnesses common in such places. No one turned away the beggars who sometimes knocked on the door asking for food.

Irene was close to her mother. Women had it hard, but few so hard as Lucia. A husband might drink or be abusive (though Dante had been a rare non-drinker, and stern but not cruel), but he could work and bring home the money. A woman without a husband might not have to worry about a man's meanness, but she would have a terrible time getting money. And people would say that she should get a man instead of working anyway, though not many men were interested in a woman with teenage children.

Up until then, her work experiences had not made her especially keen on a life of labour. Her father and uncle had worked on their knees in the mine, sometimes in cold water; she remembered how they came home with their filthy clothes frozen stiff. Now she had to help her mother with the cleaning and cooking and the sewing and laundry. Dan helped, too; unlike most boys, he could sew and cook. He was considered one of the best-dressed boys at school, though he had only two pairs of pants. He ironed them every day so that they always looked nice. Her mother took pride in this and in keeping a spotless house. Poverty was no excuse for being dirty; she had nothing but scorn for people who didn't keep clean houses.

But it was a lot of work. She didn't think of herself as a good student, but she studied hard, and that took time. For several months, she had been getting up early in the morning to help her mother unload dynamite from the trucks at the mine. Many of her relatives walked past them on their way to work, but none of them helped unload the explosives, just like none of them intervened when the office manager tried to grab her on a Saturday when she cleaned his office. It was hard to lift the heavy boxes, but they did it and went back home wheezing and gasping for breath. They all had asthma. Dante had had it too; maybe that's what killed him.

She missed her father. Life had been easier when he was alive. He had been different from the other men. He could read and write, in both English and Italian. He would translate for the workers who could not speak English and help them get their immigration papers. He was dapper and could dance up a storm, though Lucia's father had warned her about marrying a man who liked to dance so much. It was strange how Lucia would stand up to Dante, and how he, himself, had been in mortal fear of his own mother, to whom he had dutifully given his paycheck even after he was married—yet it was clear that Dante had been the "boss" of their household. She was a little afraid of Lucia, but if her father said her name in that special way, she knew she had better listen.

One thing Irene looked forward to in school was seeing her boyfriend, Bud. He was two years older and a senior in high school. He would graduate this year if he didn't play hooky too much. She felt lucky to have such a boyfriend; different, not only not Italian, but also not Catholic. Lucia did not mind this, but his parents were not so happy about her. They were strict Baptists, as quiet and reserved as the Italians were noisy and gregarious. They weren't rich, but they were better off than her family. The father had worked all through the hard times as an engineer in the glass factory. He wore a coat and tie to work and even around the house. Bud could get a job there and have a steady source of money, and that was the main thing.

Bud wanted to get married as soon as Irene finished school. She hadn't thought about saying no. If they married and he had a job, it would make it easier for her mother to get by. Maybe they could help out. If they married, her future would be secure. Plus, they would have a place of their own and could start a family. He loved kids and so did she. She knew all about keeping a house and how hard could it be to raise children. That's what women did, and she would have a good man besides. Not that she didn't have dreams about being an actress or an artist. All girls did, but dreams came true for a different class of people. For people like her, only security mattered. She just hoped that the war everyone was talking about didn't come.

Bud: my Father

NON-FICTION

Bud's feelings toward his father Carl were ambivalent. He admired his father's abilities. Though Carl had quit school in the eighth grade, he had become a time-study engineer at the plant. He could add long columns of numbers in his head and he could tell time without a watch. He had been a skilled athlete, a long-distance runner and a baseball player. He used to take Bud to the local games; Bud remembered yelling "that's my dad" when Carl hit a home run. His father's best sport was bowling. He was the best bowler in town, and he almost never missed a spare. Bud was a good bowler himself, the one sport besides pool he could play well. His high school yearbook had commented that "he could give his dad a run for his money" on the lanes. But he wasn't as good as Carl, and that was the problem. He felt that his father didn't respect him. Maybe it was because Bud had been sickly when he was a baby, with tubercular bones that had cost him two years in a sanitarium. He still wasn't strong, and he never could play baseball or any of the rougher sports. He sure wasn't much of a fighter.

The one thing Bud did have over his father was that he had been in the War. He had enlisted in the navy right after

Pearl Harbor. He had graduated from high school in 1940 and, with his father's help, started to work in the factory, packing glass into crates for fifty cents an hour. He hadn't liked school much; what was the point of studying when you could hang out with the guys. Working and earning a paycheck were all right, though the work was monotonous. He had been to a Civilian Conservation Corps camp two summers before, so he was used to getting up early and working hard. He wasn't a troublemaker or a loudmouth, and that helped too. Most of his classmates were either working or had turned in applications, so he had friends at work, which was nice. It was strange at first, going through the long tunnel and into the enormous plant, punching the time clock and getting to work. He had started at the south end, where the unskilled assembly work was done, but he hoped to get a better job, maybe in one of the shops or at the north end where they made the specialty glass. Right before he had started to work there, the men had organized a union, and now they didn't have to take all the crap the foremen had handed out before; at least, that's what the old-timers told him. He had heard more than a few unkind comments about Carl from the men, though they had a grudging respect for his athletic skills. But they didn't like his stopwatch, timing their every move and motion, always trying to make them work faster and harder. Carl was a "company man," something Bud could not afford to be. For his father it was "PPG this and PPG that." For him, it was just a job, though he couldn't see why you shouldn't put in a good day's work for your pay.

Everyone in the town had been talking about war. It sounded exciting, a chance to get away and do something different. Almost every guy he knew had enlisted. Not only had he joined the navy, but right after boot camp, he married his high school sweetheart. Irene had lived with her mother, Lucia, during the war and made a little money working in the company store. Everything boomed then; he remembered the crowded streets and bars the one time he went on leave before shipping out. Some bastards had made a lot of money, cheating the servicemen by raising their prices. Bud hated people like that, guys who'd get ahead whatever the cost. After boot camp, he went to radio school in Chicago. Some nights he had guard duty in front of the Chicago Stadium. Only later did he learn that inside, people were helping to develop the atomic bomb that had, finally, brought him home.

The war had been an experience like no other; young guys thousands of miles from home, boys like him, from all over the country. He had been in the Ellice Islands in the South Pacific for two years. He remembered the odor of the bodies piled up on the beach of the island on which he was stationed. You could smell them from 10,000 feet up in the plane; it was a smell that stayed with him still. Later, he watched U.S. marines pick the gold out of the dead men's teeth before they were dumped into mass graves. He remembered getting bombed every night; one of his bunk mates had been hit in the middle of the night without him even knowing it. The radio operators listened to Tokyo Rose, and she would tell them that they were going to be hit that night. She "interviewed" American prisoners of war, and one night he heard the voice of a soldier from his hometown. He wrote back to his wife to tell the parents that their son was alive. He never made better friends than his buddies in the war.

When he got back home, he returned to work. He lived with his wife and Lucia for a year. That had been awful, with no hot water and an outhouse, not to mention the coal smoke and foul air. After their son was born, they moved to a small house on a farm, closer to work but still a long walk, and still an outhouse. The excitement of the war had made it difficult to go back to the factory. You just didn't want to take any shit from the boss after you had seen so much death. The war had made him and his buddies men, and they wanted to be treated like men. There had been confrontations and strikes, but now at least it looked as though the company had learned that it couldn't run them over. The war had changed his view of Carl a little. His father hadn't been there and done what Bud had done. And his parents hadn't been so nice to his wife, either. They'd actually sold the car he'd bought right before the war and kept the money. His car and his money!

What kept him going was his own family. All through the war he had sent pictures of babies he'd cut out of magazines back home to Irene. Now he was a father, and he wanted things so his family could have a good life. He wanted lots of kids, too. He had begun to do a little planning. It didn't look like the Depression was going to come back. Work was steady; you could put in a lot of overtime. Funny, at least he had told Irene that he was working overtime when, instead, he had been playing cards for money after work. She caught him, and that ended that. Well, he'd take the overtime and put a little money aside. The government was giving low-interest mortgages to GIs, and he was thinking about building a house on a hill above the town. People said he was crazy to take such a risk, but he thought that it would be worth it to have a place of his own, with a big yard for his kids to play. A house with indoor plumbing and a fireplace; that would be something. Maybe he would take a correspondence course and go into radio repair. He was a radioman, after all; he knew about radios, and everybody had one. He had bought a used Hallicrafter shortwave in Texas, where he had been stationed after he left the South Pacific. He could practise on that. He would make everyone, including his father, see that he was no ordinary guy.

At the Factory Gate

NON-FICTION

I f I had some money, I would walk down the steep path to town, landing on Seventh Avenue, past the row houses and small neat homes, and make my way to Petroleum Sales. My eyes gleamed in anticipation, for this was a store filled with a child's delights: gumballs, exotic stamps, airplane kits, baseball cards, and fake cigarettes that smoked when you blew into them. These cigarettes were a special favorite of mine. With one of them dangling out of the corner of my mouth, I could pretend that I was a tough guy hanging around my uncle's dairy store looking cool and hard in jeans hung low on my hips, held up with a thin pink belt. Once in the alley behind the school yard, "Scoop" Folta, dazzling in his sunglasses and DA haircut, actually asked me for a cigarette. "Got a weed?" he asked. I felt for a moment that maybe we could be friends, but then I shamefacedly remembered that my cigarette wasn't real.

Bald old Mr. Ringler kept a sharp eye out for youthful thieves, but they didn't have trick mirrors and store dicks in that poor town, so you could pocket a treasure or two if you were careful. Mean-faced Mr. Ringler. I never minded stealing his trinkets. He wore a suit and he looked like my dad's bosses. He was rich. Probably a Jew. Surely he would never miss a set of triangle stamps from Monaco or a baseball or a pack of those cigarettes.

Petroleum Sales was in the middle of a block on Fifth Avenue, between 7th and 8th streets. On leaving, I always turned left toward the stores downtown. I might be a little apprehensive because my pal Jack's mother could come stumbling drunk and disheveled out of the side door of the bar at the Fifth Avenue Hotel. Slobbering, toothless, and in a flimsy housecoat, she would babble out some wild tale, trying all the while to grab and kiss you. More than once Jack and I witnessed this together. He would swear and tell her to get the hell home. I would pretend not to notice, and we never talked about it. Jack liked me, and I was glad for that. I knew he liked me because he invited me home even when his mother was there.

Oh, I saw some terrible scenes. At eighth-grade graduation, our parents were invited to a communion breakfast after morning mass. Jack's mother came in a pretty dress and wearing makeup, trying hard to make small talk and mingle among the parents unnoticed. But no one except my mother would speak to her. Poor woman. She was like an old and broken plate, shoddily glued together and with all of the cracks showing. We waited for her to break, the meaner among us snickering as her voice rose and her speech thickened. The nuns shared knowing glances with the parents, secretly blaming Jack for the sins of his mother. Funny how these angels of mercy had so little compassion for those who needed it and how easily they were impressed by the material things they had forsaken. Finally she announced, almost in a shout, that she had to go home to turn off the stove. We watched her leave in silence and then returned to our eggs and toast, basking in the glow of our parent's pride. All but Jack. He had no appetite. Tonight there would be a violent argument. His mother would screech at his bookkeeper father. Jack's dad could add faster than a calculator, but he didn't have speed enough to avoid the flying shoes and the screams of "Eddie, you bastard!" "Eddie, you cocksucker!"

When I think of Jack's mother, I remember something she told my grandma Lucia. Grandma was working at Greenbaum's department store, and one day she was accosted by Jack's two aunts who tried to sell her some pies that they had just bought on sale at the supermarket. Jack's mother sidled up to my grandmother and said, sotto voce, "You have to watch out for my sisters. They're crazy."

The Fifth Avenue Hotel was a three-story gray tenement, buttressed by fire escapes. It was home to an assortment of derelicts, old bachelors, and shady deals. Through the side door oozed the cool, sickening smells of dirt and stale beer. Ceiling fans muted the sodden chatter of the barflies and petty racketeers who drank away the afternoons there. I longed to walk in and order a Coke or ask for change for the pinball machine. Maybe Ruben or Shannon or Jumbo Lawrence would say, "How's it going kid?" On the other hand, crazy Johnny Luscatoff might goose me, or the gangster bartender, Pauly DiRenzo, might tell me to get the fuck out. So, I never did go in. Instead, I turned left on 9th Street and headed for the park. If it was early, I might cross the street to look longingly at the gobs in the window of Kunst's bakery. Later, when I learned that "kunst" means "art" in German, I had fantasies about the bakery: I imagined fancy breads shaped and ornamented to look like Picasso's harlequins and a banner with huge, sensuous letters cut out of construction paper that said "Cakes decorated by Matisse." Mr. Kunst could have made a fortune.

The park took up a whole block, between 9th and 8th Streets and 4th and 3rd Avenues, a pretty park and large, too, for a small town, with a bandstand in the middle, just right for patriotic speeches on Memorial Day and the Fourth of July. Near the bandstand was the flag-bedecked statue of John Ford, the town's founder. On a summer day, women would watch over their children from the park benches conveniently

located along the walkways and under the tall trees. At one
corner of the park, across the street from the factory gate,
pensioners would play checkers and talk, some smiling because their days as working stiffs were over and some wist-
ful because they were locked out of their second home. In
1957, the park was a peaceful place. But a dozen years later,
when my classmates trooped back from Vietnam, time bombs,
bearded and wearing peace signs on their olive drab fatigues,
the park became a war zone. We desecrated the flag, smoked
dope, painted our faces, and fought with the police. The park
was ours, and who could blame the matrons and retirees for
seeking shelter elsewhere.

I have always been obsessed with being on time, so I usually arrived at the park twenty or thirty minutes before shift
change. I had come to town to meet my father at the factory
gate. To kill time, I would walk around and through the park,
chewing on a toothpick and daydreaming. If no one was looking, I would practise my pitching motion, kicking my right leg
high like Warren Spahn, but quickly shifting into calling the
play-by-play. If you can picture this, you'll understand why
the neighbors said that they could always pick me out at a distance by the way I walked.

At about five minutes to four, I would try to get a seat on
one of the benches near the Works 6 gate, which was located
across from the northwest corner of the park, and wait for the
whistle to blow. Strung out along the river, from the bridge at
the lower end of town to 13th street, over a mile in all, the factory was divided into three units. Works 4, the largest, was one
long assembly line, starting at the Batch House where sand,
cullet, chemicals, and the other ingredients used to make glass
were mixed and cooked, to G&P where the finished plates of
glass were ground and polished. From Shop 2 came the jour-
neymen who did the factory's carpentry, painting, electrical
repair, and general maintenance; it was here, too, that appren-
tices learned the various trades. Finally, at the northern end

of the factory, was Works 6, where my father worked. Works 6 was special because, there, the glass was still made in small batches, by skilled workers. Huge kettles of molten glass were cooked and poured by hand, and then the plates were cut into basketball bank boards or aircraft windshields so thin that they could be bent. The men who cooked the glass worked irregular stints, sometimes doing a double shift, sometimes coming out in the middle of the night, and sometimes just sitting around waiting for the spectacular pouring of the glass. They had a kitchen outfitted with stove and refrigerator, and they weren't very friendly to strangers. At that time my father was an examiner, although he had had many different jobs, from lowly packer to skilled cutter. He checked the plates for flaws in front of a high-intensity lamp in a dark room; rejecting those pieces with more than a certain number. He told me that the company didn't like to ship bad glass, but the foremen weren't happy when he rejected too many plates. That was a company for you.

My father was a precise man, but not as precise as his father, who also worked at Number 6. Well, grandpa wasn't actually a worker. The truth is, he had been a time-study engineer, a regular Frederick Taylor who worshipped efficiency and the piece-rate. I admired my grandfather, mostly because he was such a good bowler, but I didn't quite trust him. He wore a suit and tie, always, like Mr. Ringler. My father never wore a suit and tie, and he never went to church on Sunday. Grandpa tithed at the Baptist Church and supported Temperance and the Republican Party. He voted against Roosevelt four times. But my distrust was small by comparison to that of my father's work mates. They hated grandpa's stopwatch and always slowed down when he made his rounds. I wonder if his son did, too.

I got excited when the whistle blew. The gate faced 3rd Avenue, but it was at the end of a long tunnel under the railroad tracks, so it would be a couple of minutes before anyone came out. Maybe Jack's aunts, who spent eight hours sitting in a dimly lit room checking thin pieces of optical glass and who that morning could have been seen flying down the street to punch in at 7:59, would be the first to surface. Or, more likely, it would be the slackers like Frank Swain, who always got to the time clock first. Then small groups of three or four, some smoking and backslapping, others sullen and pensive, would stream steadily up the steps and onto the street. A human machine, breaking into its component parts that, as if by magic, decomposed into solitary faces. I looked for people I knew. Roy, with a plate in his head. Moe, the union vice president. Dom, a premature greaser with a Harley and an armful of tattoos. Nick, my dad's best friend, a solid, heavy-set Russian with a sly sense of humor. I liked those men, but my father was the main attraction. He would be in the middle of a row of buddies, smoking a Lucky Strike. So handsome with his jet-black hair, perfectly parted and always in place, his shirt smartly tucked into his creased trousers. Many of the men had potbellies and wore old-fashioned caps, but he was slim and bareheaded. He never had a five o'clock shadow, and his shoes were always bright and shiny. And while Dom might smell so strongly of sweat that it was hard to breathe, dad always smelled as if his clothes had just come off the drying line. He was sharper, finer, and I was proud that he was my father.

When I saw him, I would wave to catch his attention and then walk over to join the exodus. His buddies might pat me on the head and say, "Bud, is that your boy?" or "Hi, Mike," or "Boy, he's getting big." When we got to his black '51 Chevy, we'd say goodbye to his friends. Someone would surely say, "See you at work." We'd get into the car. I'd show him my booty, but I wouldn't tell him how I got it. He'd offer me a stick of Beechnut gum, and we'd drive home.

II.
The Seeds of Consciousness

Class: A Personal Story

NON-FICTION

I was born in 1946 in a small mining village in western Pennsylvania, about forty miles north of Pittsburgh, along a big bend in the Allegheny River. The house in which I lived during my first year of life had neither hot water nor indoor plumbing. It was a company house, and my grandmother had purchased it for $1,000 from the mining corporation after the town had ceased to be a company town, thanks to the United Mine Workers. A small coal stove in the living room heated the entire house.

My grandmother came to this town in the mid-1930s to be close to relatives after her husband died. She and her two children—my mother and my uncle—lived in the small, tarpaper-shingled house, and she eked out a living in a place with few job opportunities for women. Most of the miners were Italian; Italian was more or less the town's lingua franca. Miners everywhere show unusual cohesion and solidarity and have often been among the shock troops of labour movements. The common ethnicity of these miners deepened their fraternity. However, mining was considered men's work, and Italians were typical Latin male chauvinists; women were to raise children and take care of the household. My grandma's parents had taken in boarders, and grandma had learned women's work, including helping to stir the enormous batches of polenta made every day to feed the men. Now she had a hard time finding work. She cleaned the town doctor's house, took in laundry, and mended clothes. She and her children got jobs unloading dynamite at the mine site.

There was a degree of spontaneous class consciousness in the village. During the Great Depression, everyone was in the same boat: poor and in need of work. People were generous with one another; when beggars came to the door, the miners fed them. When the union arrived, the men were nearly unanimous in their support. During strikes, no one scabbed. The Catholic Church exerted a conservative influence, but priests in poor towns are often sympathetic to workers and their families. The town's physical isolation helped to insulate workers from the hegemonic forces at work in the larger society. Italians already had a long history of radical agitation in the United States, strengthened by the strong prejudice they faced.

Both my mother and grandma developed some sense of belonging to the working class. However, this was not a consciousness that would lead to collective actions. Their main concern was their immediate family. After her children were grown, grandma took a number of jobs. She was a cook on a tugboat that pushed barges loaded with steel from Pittsburgh to New Orleans. She worked as a governess for the very rich in Manhattan and Pittsburgh. She cooked in a restaurant. She understood the inferior position of wage labourers. But only individual acts of rebellion were available to her, as when she shamed the rich woman who employed her, saying that she didn't work for her because she liked her but because she needed the money. The strict and oppressive gender division of labour she had seen and experienced since childhood made the kind of solidarity that builds a labour movement unlikely. Of course, my grandma was not alone in this. Tens of millions of women could have helped create stronger labour movements than the ones actually built and, unfortunately, the same is still true today.

The Second World War brought the mining village out of the Depression. It also helped to assimilate many Italian-Americans into the more conservative American mainstream. After the war, nationalism and anti-communism became much stronger, and individual acquisitiveness began to replace the more communal life of the pre-war era. The union of mine-workers became a place where a few miners could move up the economic ladder. As the national union declined and lost its militancy under the corrupt leadership of Tony Boyle, the local's leaders became Boyle stalwarts. Within a few years, the mine itself was closed, and miners and their children began to move from the town or found work at other mines, in construction, or in factories up and down the river. People renovated their houses; the one in which I was born was one of the few remaining with its original tar-paper shingles. The townsfolk gradually joined the post-war mainstream, gaining some in material goods but losing most of the collective character of the earlier village.

What values did I assimilate from the mining town? This is a complicated question. The working class solidarity always shown by underground miners seeped into my consciousness, as did the ethnic clannishness of the Italian immigrants. This meant a certain distrust of anyone with money and authority and anyone outside the community. But these incipient seeds of class consciousness were counteracted by other, more troubled feelings. Mining towns in the United States were typically owned by the mining companies, which exerted a near totalitarian control over the residents. They owned the houses, the only store (the infamous "company store"), all utilities, the schools, the library—everything. They had their own private police—the Coal and Iron Police in Pennsylvania—sanctioned by state law. The climate in such a town is one of perpetual insecurity and fear, emotions compounded by the danger of the work in the mines. While such authoritarian rule generates anger and hate, it also gives rise to feelings of inadequacy and worthlessness. Misery is one's lot in life. There must be something wrong with us. Those in power must have special abilities and powers we don't have. We deserve our fate. Organized religion contributes to this sense of helplessness and shifts attention away from material conditions and toward God and the afterlife.

Poverty and social isolation added fuel to the fire of fear. People lacked self-confidence and had deep-seated feelings of inferiority. When kids from the village went to the high school in the factory town three miles upriver, they faced a mocking condescension. They had the wrong clothes. They were greasy "dagos." They were "dumb coal miners." Some, like one of my cousins, reacted with rage; he hung a teacher from a third floor window for calling him a dumb coal miner. But others took it to heart and were scarred forever.

It is difficult to overstate the power of fear and poverty in shaping how working men and women think and act. Fear of losing a job. Fear of not finding a job. Fear of being late with bill payments. Fear of the boss's wrath. Fear your house might burn down. Fear your kids will get hurt. I inherited these emotions. I have a PhD and have always had a job that brings forth instant respect from others. Yet, I lack confidence and am anxious in the face of authority. I can confront the powerful in a group, even if I am a leader of it, but as an individual, I hate any kind of confrontation with authority and always wonder if I have the right to confront. I prefer to remain in the background, to be invisible.

As working class men and women are sucked into the capitalist milieu, they try to make sure that their children do not end up like them. They sacrifice so that the kids can exit the working class and become entrepreneurs and professionals. This can have painful results. If the children are successful, they may come to be ashamed of their parents, and their parents may come to resent them. These feelings may never be explicitly stated, but will show themselves, sometimes, in not so subtle ways. A successful child who marries a person from outside the working class will hesitate to visit home as often as in the past. Children might blame parents for not giving them the advantages their spouses, new friends, and coworkers take for granted. Parents will be proud of their successful children, but at the same time might resent their children's new lifestyles, which stand in sharp contrast to their own. A child's big house, professional spouse, fancy car, and the grandchildren's private schools seem to mock the way they themselves live. I remember arguing with my father. He said to me, "You read too much." I shot back, "If you'd read a book once in awhile instead of getting all your information from television, maybe you'd be better off."

Ambivalence marks the emotions of the working class. In a society where worth is measured by money, the lack of money signifies a lack of worth. However, daily life, including religion, tells workers that there is more to a person's character than money. It also tells them that money is often tainted with corruption and violence. There is a man from the mining village who became wealthy. People love to talk about how he was one of the poorest persons in the town and now owns many businesses and several mansion-like homes. He is a friendly fellow and generous to his family and friends. On the one hand, those who "knew him when" now bask reflectively in his glory. It is quite a thing to get invited to his house, and those who are will regale you with descriptions of the grounds and furnishings. However, not far below the surface, there is a sense that this man has come by his money illegitimately. If you suggest that perhaps, given the nature of his businesses, he was involved with organized crime, most people will not vehemently deny this. Wonder, jealousy, admiration, hatred, all mixed together in a confusing brew. The rich may be, in one interpretation, God's chosen, but then again, it is more difficult for a rich man to get into heaven than for a camel to pass through the eye of a needle.

Attitudes toward work are also ambivalent. Most working class employment sucks, and everyone knows it. And it is impossible not to be aware of the tensions existing in every workplace or to see that most bosses want only your labour, and as much of it as they can get. So workers cut corners, pretend to be working, and find unproductive ways to kill time and make the work day go faster. Yet, work is a natural human endeavor, and even the most menial job requires some ingenuity. So workers want to do a good job at the same time that they know that doing so will not necessarily be to their advantage. Doing a good job certainly did not make the job a good one, fit for a human being. My father took a dim view of slackers, but he was not above "lifting" small items from the shop that might be useful at home. I felt much the same way when I was a full-time college teacher. As our work became more alienating, many of us began to cut corners—refusing to give essay examinations, shortening classes, especially the long evening lectures, and getting the "take-a-day" flu as often as we dared. I didn't like to see teachers slacking even though I could understand it and did it myself.

The attitude of working class youth toward school mirrors their parents' ambivalence toward success and work. Schools are oppressive places, and kids naturally rebel against the agents of this oppression: teachers and administrators. When I was in school, most boys were destined to be future factory workers. Only a few were deemed mentally fit to succeed in college. In the minds of most pupils, these few were the enemy as much as were the teachers. "Ordinary" students knew instinctively that they were not going to "succeed," so they built defense mechanisms to make this understanding less painful. It was not "manly" to do well in school. Physical toughness was the mark of a real man. A scholar was like a girl, who could be smart but wasn't likely to succeed in any event. At the same time, the "brains" had to be respected; the success of the few was the other side of the coin of their "failure." A student who did well could be admired and hated at the same time. From the point of view of the rulers of the economic system, the schools have been great successes. Only a few working class youth are needed to fill the relatively few skilled labour slots in the workplace. The values absorbed by the rest of the working class boys and girls will fit them very well for the work they will do and make it difficult to blame anyone but themselves for their failure to escape their class.

When I was two, my family moved from the mining village to a small house on a farm about three miles east of the factory town where my father worked. We had hot water but still had to use an outhouse. Dad often walked to work; it would be a couple of years before we got a car. Three years later, my parents took advantage of the government-backed home loans that were so important to the development of the white suburbs and the demise of urban, working class culture. There was another child now, my sister, and the four of us moved into a three-bedroom house with modern conveniences on a large lot. This is where my four siblings and I grew up. There weren't many houses nearby when we moved, but over the next two decades, a few hundred more were built as workers began to live the "American Dream" in the post-war "American Century."

The town was small, not quite 10,000 residents at its peak, but it housed the biggest plate glass factory in the world. There was also a large pottery, right next to the glass factory. The city of Pittsburgh was a centre of glass manufacturing, and the owner of the town's factory was the Pittsburgh Plate Glass Company. Everyone just called it "PPG." The factory was many blocks long and took up in width what would have been the town's first two avenues. Inside, there was a workforce divided along several dimensions. Most of the workers were relatively unskilled, but there were a significant number of craft workers, some of whom still made glass without assembly line mechanization and some of whom were tradesmen, such as carpenters, millwrights, and electricians. The workers were mostly men, but there were large numbers of women in certain departments, like the one in which optical glass was examined. There were also black workers, who, as was typical in northern factories, were locked into unskilled jobs with little chance of advancement. There were no Asian workers and few Hispanics.

Until the workers unionized the plant in the late 1930s, the company ran the town; it was as much a company town as the mining village. But it was larger and more complex. There was a more nuanced class structure: not just workers, foremen, and absentee owners, but also shopkeepers and professionals.

Reflecting divisions in the workplace, the townspeople were also divided. While nearly everyone in the mining town was Catholic, people in the factory town practised many Protestant faiths as well. There were a few Jews, mainly shopkeepers and professionals. Catholics faced a certain amount of discrimination in that they were unlikely to become top managers in the glass plant; these slots were reserved for those in the mainstream Protestant denominations. Anti-Semitism was widespread, although Jews were, for the most part, tolerated. They couldn't join certain clubs and they were called vicious names, but at the same time, they were grudgingly admired for their economic success.

The ethnic and racial makeup of the town most differentiated it from the mining village. There was no "melting pot." Whites were rigidly separated from blacks, but whites themselves were not a uniform group. Besides religious differences, there were important ethnic splits. Those with northern European ancestries were more likely to hold supervisory positions in the plant, and there was considerable bigotry expressed by them against Italian-Americans and those from

Eastern Europe. These prejudices were aligned with religious animosities as well, since the Anglo-Saxons were typically protestant, and the "Hunkies," Polacks," and "Dagos" were Catholic. I remember my father disdainfully telling me how the kids in these groups had their heads shaved for the summer. It was not uncommon for parents to discourage their children, especially their daughters, from dating anyone from the "wrong" ethnic groups.

Too much should not be made of ethnic (and religious) differences, however. Even by my early childhood, these had begun to break down, and cross-ethnic marriages were common. Inter-ethnic class solidarity was evident in the glass workers' union, both in strikes and in the union's internal politics. For many years, the president of the local was an Arab-American, who rose to become a national officer.

The one divide that was never breached was that of race. There was a small black community in the town, segregated at the southern or "lower" end. People there had their roots in the rural south and had, for the most part, come north in the great migration following the First World War. Many of the men found work in the glass factory and pottery, though always in the least skilled and most onerous jobs. While white persons did associate with their black townsfolk—some poor whites also lived in the "lower" end, whites and blacks played sports together, there was no segregation in the schools—close relationships were rare. Black workers could not aspire to union office, nor could black citizens hope to win local political office. Racial epithets were always ready to come out of the mouths of white persons. It was a rare conversation in a bar or club that did not include these. A fair number of whites seemed obsessed with black people, never missing a chance to denigrate them or blame them for whatever the whites perceived as bad. It was definitely taboo for whites and blacks of the opposite sex to socialize too closely, much less date or marry.

What effects did life in the factory town have on class consciousness? In many respects, these were the same as in the mining village. Workers generally disdained their bosses but had the same ambivalence toward "a fair day's work" as did the miners. But the factory had a more complex hierarchy of jobs than did the mine, so workers could aspire to better jobs, including the job of foreman or first-level supervisor. Since the company had some control over who got the jobs covered by union contract and complete control over who became a supervisor, a worker might think that it would be better not to oppose the company too overtly or militantly. The company could also use co-optation to weaken class solidarity, draining off the most thoughtful workers into management.

The factory town also had a range of small businesses, and a worker could aim for the petty bourgeoisie. My uncle once opened a small restaurant with a fellow worker in an effort to escape the factory and be his own boss. My father had hopes of becoming a radio repairman and later took a correspondence school course to learn drafting. This kind of thinking and acting, while easy to understand, also sapped class consciousness.

As with the miners, the Second World War profoundly affected the ways in which workers thought and acted. On the one hand, the factory men came home from the war unwilling to tolerate the corporate despotism their fathers had suffered before unionization. They struck and filed grievances and won more control over what went on at work than they ever could have imagined before the war. I well remember the two summers I worked in the plant. My grandfather, a time-study engineer, got me a summer job while I was in college. I did mostly clerical work, cataloguing accidents and analyzing accident reports to see where and when they were most likely to occur. Many children of workers got such jobs, and the company found this a good way to recruit local college kids into management (as with the miners, parents had mixed feelings about this but in general were proud to help their children to get out of the working class).

My job was housed in the fire department—the factory was large enough to have its own. The firemen were typically on-call and often had few regular daytime duties, so they spent a lot of time drinking coffee and talking. The atmosphere was casual, and the supervisors never, while I was there, told the men to do anything. The union officers, themselves full-time union staffers (drawing pay from the company), stopped every day for coffee. The firemen moved around the plant freely and were good sources of gossip that might be useful to the union. The union president was a gruff man with one arm; he had lost the other to a grinding machine. The vice-president was a dapper man, a superlative bowler and pool player, and a chronic gambler. Conversation ranged freely from football pools to ongoing disputes with management. I was impressed with the degree of freedom that the workers and the union officers had, the product of long years of class struggle after the war in which most of them had fought. Without using the word in a sexist way, I would say that the war had made them "men," and they demanded to be treated as such.

On the other hand, the war and its aftermath locked most of these workers into mainstream America. Wars are always about getting people in one country to hate those in another. And if this can be done once, it can be done again; all that is needed is for the state to declare a new enemy. After the war, the new enemy was the Soviet Union and, by implication, all radical thinking and acting. It was no accident that the labour movement was held up as an entity infiltrated by communists and, further, that workers would have to repudiate the reds in their unions if they were to maintain membership in U.S. society. War gets people used to obeying orders issued by the state, and this habit of mind worked to good advantage from the employers' perspective when they strove to regain the power they had lost during the heyday of the Congress of

Industrial Organization (CIO). Workers who insisted on trying to deepen what the CIO had achieved before and during
the war—greater control by workers of their workplaces, a
weakening of racism, solidarity with workers in other countries, the beginnings of a social welfare state—were simply declared enemies of the state, on par with the defeated Germans
and Japanese. The workers in my hometown, never especially
radical to begin with and deeply influenced by the war and by
the Catholic Church, bought into the new patriotism of anti-
communism wholeheartedly and, in the process, never seized
the opportunity to use the new union strength to deepen their
class consciousness.

To help workers embrace the Cold War, the government
initiated a variety of programs aimed at giving them a greater
material stake in U.S. society. The most important of these
was the subsidization of home mortgages. Millions of working class families bought homes on the cheap, usually away
from the cities and towns in the new and more isolated and
diffuse suburbs. Home ownership came to define the "good
life" for workers, and the constant care and worry that had to
be devoted to home ownership left workers with little time for
anything else, except perhaps to sit around the television every night to live through the characters on the various drama
and comedy shows. An enormous amount of propaganda was
devoted (and still is) to the wonders of owning a house and the
satisfaction to be gained by living in one with a family whose
members were devoted to one another. This and the array
of consumer goods needed to maintain a home were all that
workers needed to be happy. My parents bought our house in
1950. For them this represented both a bold move and a dec-
laration that they were part of the "American Century." Their
lives devolved away from work and class solidarity toward a
more limited and insular family life.

Subsidized home ownership was restricted to whites, who
often signed covenants in which they obligated themselves

not to sell their houses to minorities. The denial of home ownership to blacks further separated the races and made interracial solidarity all the more unlikely. When I was twelve years old, I took a very large paper route, with more than one hundred customers scattered over a five-mile set of interconnected roads. Every customer lived in a single-family house; no one rented. I had no black customers.

The impact of living in the factory town on my consciousness came mainly through the schools. Like everyone else, I was in school for thousands of hours during my most formative years, so it was impossible not to be influenced by what I was and was not taught. In retrospect, it is fair to say that, in terms of what went on in the town and in the larger society, the schools were in one sense a mirror image and in another way a fantasy world. Working class boys and girls have always been cannon fodder for society's least desirable jobs, and the schools did their best to make this appear inevitable. The few with high IQs, as evidenced by their scores on tests that were designed not to measure anything of relevance about us except our skill at taking such tests, were placed in special sections and given an opportunity to escape our class or at least move into its upper reaches. The rest were consigned to courses that would prepare them to take the orders and perform the mundane tasks necessary to produce the mass consumption goods that would make them happy. It was understood that we were in our section because that is where our intelligence objectively placed us, and, for the most part, we believed this. I have no doubt that the teachers believed this as well. Not only did this separation of "smart" from "dumb" make it unlikely that students would develop a sense of solidarity, but as it became part of our self-consciousness, it also made us believe that we were ourselves responsible for our fate. I was in Section One because I was superior; you were in Section Seven because you were inferior. I would go to college because I deserved it, and you would go to the factory for the same reason. I would show the world that class was not a barrier to success. You would show everyone that you were just too lazy to deserve what I got. The fact that the kids in the lower sections were more likely to be poor and black reinforced class and race stereotypes. Teachers did nothing to discourage any of this.

The schools I attended never told us the truth about the world in which we lived, and it is in this sense that I say that they were fantasy worlds. There were two parts to the lies at the heart of my education: what the teachers told us and what they did not tell us. They told us that the United States was a kind of paradise on earth and that other countries were either inferior or evil. They told us that Christopher Columbus was a great explorer and discoverer. They told us that the people decided through their votes how the nation would be governed. But of far greater importance was what they did not tell us. Nothing about racism, nothing about American Indians, nothing about the misery foisted upon the poor nations and peoples of the world by the rich ones, nothing about progressive social movements. Nothing about the factories that dominated our town. Nothing about unions, despite the fact that nearly every man in town belonged to one. Nothing about the arts except the Shakespeare of Julius Caesar and a few other "safe" writers. Nothing but clichés and trivialities about the rest of the world. Nothing about capitalism. I cannot today remember a single inspiring lesson from my teachers. Some were nice; a couple of the science and math teachers were smart and gave us a decent background in these subjects; most were harmless. But none were scholars, and none gave me insight into the political economy that makes the world go 'round.

My high school was a public school. Before I went there, I attended a Catholic school. Here, ignorance reigned supreme, and the main goal was to suppress thinking and desire and encourage blind faith. Obedience, fear of authority, guilt—these were the staples of a Catholic education.

Naturally, some students rebelled against such an insipid
education. However, most rebellion just reinforced the social
outcomes the schools were established to guarantee. Rather
than demand that we be taught something relevant and useful—something that would help us in making a good life for
ourselves—boys and girls rebelled by cutting classes and refusing to do any work at all. This led to poor grades and
evaluations by the teachers and a ticket to a dead-end working class life.

After high school, I left the factory town for good, first to
attend college and graduate school and then to take a job as
a college teacher. I got out of the working class, at least the
industrial worker part of it. But my class background and consciousness, such as they were, followed me.

When I became a professor, I encountered new ambiva-
lences. Professors have not historically thought of themselves
as workers; if anything, they have thought themselves superior to workers and more closely aligned with society's elites.
Though professors might disdain the bourgeoisie, they would
no doubt prefer to dine with a successful businessman than a
ditch digger.

So here I was in an elite job, fulfilling my parents' hope
that I wouldn't be a factory worker. But I was among "colleagues"—an odd word for me—who had little knowledge
of or sympathy with working people. If I was to succeed on
this new job, I would have to take on the habits of mind and
behavior of the other professors, thinking and acting in ways
alien to the lives of my parents and the residents of my hometown. I would have to dress differently. I would have to curb
my instinct to use words like "fuck" and "asshole." I would
have to adopt a more impersonal style of speech. In a word, I
would have to behave.

College and graduate school had taken off some of the
rough edges of a working class youth, but they had not prepared me for what I encountered as a professor. There were

enough boys like me in college, so I could act pretty much as I did at home. It was exhilarating to be in a school where I didn't have to apologize for being smart and eager to learn, and where I was thought to be a diamond in the rough. In graduate school, I stayed to myself and hung out with friends from my hometown, which was not far away. I never learned to act like a professor.

I disliked my new environment, and I didn't fare well at first. I enjoyed teaching, especially since so many of the students were from working class families. The college was located in Johnstown, Pennsylvania, a famous old steel town, best known for the great flood of 1889, caused by the neglect of the dam at a private retreat of Pittsburgh's business elite. Johnstown was my hometown writ a little larger; when I arrived there in 1969 there were more than 12,000 steel workers at the enormous Bethlehem Steel plant and the smaller one owned by U.S. Steel. The students were a lot like me, and I felt that I could teach them some of the things I wished I had been taught. The teachers and the administrators were another matter. They seemed alien to me, pretentious and disconnected from the real world. I had to stay because I would have been drafted and very likely sent to Vietnam if I quit. But I couldn't imagine ever liking the place or prospering there. My colleagues and I didn't speak the same language. I remember one of them saying, in response to something I said that betrayed my class background, "Well, you can take Mike out of Ford City [my hometown], but you can't take Ford City out of Mike."

Although I didn't think much of the college, I was proud to be a professor. My parents wanted me to get an education and a professional job and sacrificed so that I could. And I didn't want to live in my hometown or work in the factory. By nineteen, I knew that I wanted to continue studying, and by the time I began to teach, I had gone far beyond my parents and nearly all of the townspeople in terms of what I knew. My

values, too, were different than theirs. I had scrapped religion
and patriotism. This created some tension and some guilt.
I tried to live in both worlds. The college hired some good
teachers in the early 1970s, and I became friendly with them.
They seemed more knowledgeable and sophisticated—I took
crash courses of self-education in music, literature, and art
so that I could hold my own in conversations. Then I would
go to my parents' home on weekends and go to the racetrack
with friends and my father's factory buddies. This was my way
of saying that I was still a regular guy.

One of the best things about being a college teacher is that
you have time to read and reflect. And teaching is the best way
to learn. You cannot explain ideas to others unless you know
them well yourself. The war in Vietnam had forced me to think
about my beliefs. The drug-sodden and shattered friends returning to my hometown from the war belied the propaganda
of the government. My own life and that of my students put
the lie to the mainstream economics I had learned and was
teaching. I couldn't ignore this. Once you embark upon an
intellectual life, you want to know why things are happening
and you want to make sense of your own life.

My thinking was forever changed in an incident that I
describe in an essay later, so won't repeat here. I never taught
the same way again. After that day, I moved steadily to the left
and became a radical, which helped me find a way back to the
working class. To see the profound and systemic inequality in
my society meant that I had to try to change things. Intellectual
understanding is a form of hypocrisy if it isn't matched by
action. If I was no longer a member of the working class, I
could ally myself with it, actively. I could help workers to organize unions. I could help them with individual grievances.
I could teach workers. I could abandon traditional academic professional development and write for workers. I could
even try to re-conceptualize professors as workers, something that became easier as I witnessed teaching becoming

more like other jobs as administrators began running the colleges like businesses and treating the professors more like replaceable employees.

Minstrel Show

NON-FICTION

My first year in high school began in the fall of 1959. That great decade, the sixties, was soon to begin, but it was still the fifties in my home town—the boring, conservative, celebrate-America fifties. The racist fifties. Just five years before, Emmett Till had been murdered in Mississippi, dumped into the Tallahatchie River with his head bashed in and a seventy pound exhaust fan tied around his neck with barbed wire. Just three years before, during the bus boycott in Montgomery, Alabama, United States Senator James O. Eastland of Mississippi had this to say about black people:

> In every stage of the bus boycott we have been oppressed and degraded because of black, slimy, juicy, unbearably stinking niggers...African flesh-eaters. When in the course of human events it becomes necessary to abolish the Negro race, proper methods should be used. Among these are guns, bows and arrows, slingshots and knives.... All whites are created equal with certain rights, among these are life, liberty and the pursuit of dead niggers.

Neither I nor my classmates in Ford City knew anything about such matters.

I was apprehensive about high school. I had spent the past six years in a small Catholic school, and, although I did not like the nuns and their regimentation, at least I had known all my classmates. The sisters did their best to make conformists out of us: teachers had to be obeyed, as did priests, and parents. Independent thinking was dangerous, the work of the devil. Our eighth-grade teacher, Sister Herman Joseph, made memorization the sole basis of our learning. We would write down terms on the left-hand side of our notebook pages, and she would dictate the appropriate definitions for us to write on the right-hand side. Then we would stand around the room, and she would read out a definition. If you got it right, you kept standing; if you missed, you sat down. Grades were based on how many rounds you remained standing. She had me keep the grade records, so I got to sit down at all times, and I also always got the first question. I had a good memory, so even if I had not studied, I could memorize all the answers by the time it was my turn again. Getting a good grade was simple for me. Learning anything worthwhile was another matter. The Sister's definition for the radical Tom Paine was "As great an infidel as Voltaire." Not that I learned anything about Tom Paine (or Voltaire) in high school. Nor did any teacher at any level think it worthwhile to teach us about Emmett Till or Senator Eastland. However, a biology professor in college, a Catholic priest, did tell us that if a white woman had a black baby, you knew that there was a "nigger in the woodpile."

At least Herman Joseph didn't beat us when we got the wrong answer. I still wince when I think of how her predecessor had banged a girl's head against the blackboard because she confused inches, feet, and yards. Perhaps this was teacher's way of preparing her to obey her husband; learn what he wanted or you'll get the thrashing you deserve. In any event, I had the highest grade average in the school, but Sister would not allow me to get the traditional award medal. She said that I learned too easily. Rewards went only to those who endured the appropriate suffering.

On my first day in high school, my homeroom teacher, who also taught Latin, called out the roll, and when she got to me, yelled out "Melvin Yapp." This set my classmates into howls of laughter. She had glanced down at the last name on another roster, but some of my friends called me "Melvin" for quite a while. Then there was science class, taught by a heavyset farmer (he really did have a farm) with a beet-red face and a penchant for looking up girls' dresses. I hated this class, especially after the teacher knocked a student clear out of his seat for talking. I feared mightily that this would happen to me. Two older students, repeating the class after failing it the year before, sat beside and behind me. They were always making fun of me. They would ask, "Getting any?" (meaning sex), but I was so naive that for a long time I thought that they were saying, "Git ninny," which made no sense at all. When I looked at them dumbfounded, they would almost fall down laughing. The teacher was always picking on them, mocking their inability or unwillingness to learn the material. If I so much as smiled when this happened, both of them would hit me when the teacher's back was turned. Then, for at least a month, the two of them would grab me in the hall after class and drag me in the opposite direction of my next class, punching my arms and twisting my wrists. Since they were bigger than I and there were two of them, physical confrontation seemed out of the question. So I hit upon an alternative strategy, one that I used successfully throughout high school.

I was a bright kid. My mother encouraged me to read, and I did, everything from encyclopedias to novels to comic books. But being smart is not an unalloyed virtue in a place in which most young people are going to be factory workers or otherwise employed in jobs that do not require much formal education. If you stand out too much intellectually, you run the risk of social isolation and physical and verbal abuse. Luckily I was good at sports, too, especially baseball, which my father had me playing with much older kids by the age of six. He coached a youth team for boys nine through twelve, and he would bring me to the practices. I would take my turn at bat, and he would throw the ball pretty hard. If it hit me, I'd be too ashamed to cry; it wouldn't be the manly thing to do. Sports helped me, then, to develop strength and toughness. Nothing was more admired among men than sports ability and fighting prowess, and at least I had the former. I had an absolute aversion to fighting, and, most remarkably, I made it through high school without getting into a single scuffle. I did this by making special efforts to befriend the roughest boys. In the science class, I began to let the two bullies copy from me on the weekly quizzes. This helped them to pass and showed them that I had some courage. Soon the punches and the hallway abductions stopped; by the end of the year, the three of us were almost buddies.

I perfected this strategy over my years in high school. I walked to school and arrived long before classes started. I would wait in one of the stairwells for the kids who hung out there, guys from the shop classes who smoked cigarettes and were not afraid to fight. We'd talk about sports or about teachers or I'd just listen. After awhile they'd think of me as a friendly and harmless person, but one who might be useful to them. In my sophomore math class, I helped some of the basketball players get through algebra. I didn't like science classes, so later I enrolled in the regular physics class instead of the college prep course. This worked out well; I found the work easy, and so assisted the other students. That way no one would think that I considered myself better because I was smarter. Unfortunately, the teacher forced me to transfer into the more advanced class. Outside school, besides baseball, I learned how to bowl and shoot pool with skill; things "regular guys" did. I also learned to prepare for each class during the one before. That way I never had to do homework, showing my disdain for school and impressing my classmates.

The ninth grade students were divided into seven sections. Students were placed into these according to performance on standardized tests and perhaps upon the demands of the more aggressive parents. These examinations were culturally biased and in no way measured our potential abilities. So it is no wonder that no black boys or girls were enrolled in the first three sections, the ones in which the students presumably had some chance of furthering their educations. About five to ten percent of my class was black, and it was in high school that I had my first encounters with black people. Not in my classes, because I was in the first section and this was lily-white, composed disproportionately of children from more middle class (i.e., not factory worker) families. As I got to know my black classmates, it seemed to me that they were as smart as anyone else, but somehow they often had problems with their studies and, in general, the students and the teachers did not think that they were capable of good work. When a black student did excel in school, people would wonder in amazement how this could have happened.

Racism was such a fact of life that it was taken for granted. I never remember saying anything derogatory about any black person just because he or she was black. But in this I was probably exceptional, because guys were always commenting on the "niggers" or "coons" or "jungle bunnies." It was inconceivable that a white girl would date a black boy, and if she did, she would forever after be dismissed as a slut. "She fucks niggers" was pretty much the same as "She has the plague" or "She has sex with animals." The boy would have to watch his back, because this was a reason for violence. And though I did not use racial epithets, I never missed an episode of *"Amos and Andy"* on television. We were forever talking about this show, much the way people more recently talked about *"Seinfeld."* We would laugh about the outrageously stereotyped behavior of the show's characters, implicitly accepting the idea that this was the way black people really did act. We would imitate the voices of the gullible "Andy," the slow-witted janitor, "Lightin'" and the con man "Kingfish." We would memorize lines, and I can remember some of them still.

The implication of all this was that we considered black people as an exotic species; they were not like us. They existed to make us laugh and to thrill us with their athletic prowess. Black women were thought of as over-sexed. People would say, "You're not a man until you've split the black oak" (had sex with a black woman). No one challenged this kind of talk; to do so would mark you as a "nigger lover." Yet it was not necessarily bad to have black friends, as long as you understood that you were white. We suffered amazing delusions about the feelings of black persons. One of my good friends worked in his father's combination convenience store and gas station, located at the "lower end" of town. He was our expert on black life; he knew nearly every black person in town. We'd listen intently as he'd tell us about black folks, about the fat whore who lived at the "Blue Goose" hotel, about the foolishness of the slow-witted "Dewey," about the strange antics of the sickly brother of the town's best basketball player. He said in a tone of superiority that he could call our black classmates "niggers" because he knew them so well. A few years later, I was drinking with a friend in a bar in a mean Pittsburgh neighborhood. We had just bought a milkshake glass full of gin for a woman who said that it was her birthday. We were the only white persons in the place, and my companion, an obese ex-sailor, started to talk about "niggers." I told him to shut up; that kind of talk could get us killed. He said, "Don't worry; they know me here."

I disliked all my ninth grade classes except English. Latin was difficult and boring. Fortunately, our teacher was often sick, and the substitute knew nothing about languages, living or dead. Civics was taught by an old woman who believed that it was important for us to know every detail of the mechanics of every level of government. Maybe she was right, but this material was as dry as dust to me. I've already mentioned the science class. I don't know which was worse, the teacher's brutality or the way he'd say, "Please, you people," when we got on his nerves. I didn't mind algebra. It was taught by one of the school's legendary basketball players, and he made it interesting, telling us little tidbits like the Arabic root of the word "algebra." But my favorite class was English, which was taught by our favorite teacher, Mr. Conlon, or "Skinny."

Skinny was one of those teachers who seems like "one of the guys" to the students. He'd tell us jokes and let us in on some of the gossip of the school, the things that went on between the teachers and between them and the staff. This was an extraordinary thing in those days when the gap between student and teacher was much wider than it is today. He had us do unusual assignments, such as spontaneous speeches on a subject he'd name on the spot. We were his "best" students, but he had to teach many of the other sections as well. That year he had to teach the Section 7 class; these students were deemed hopeless by the school, which was why they were put there in the first place. Skinny let it be known that these kids were too dumb to learn, so he had devised alternative education for them. One of his tactics was to conduct arm wrestling contests among the boys in the class. We thought that this was great stuff. Why waste your time on those who were impervious to learning, whose skulls were too thick to permeate? Better to prepare them for the hard manual labour that they were no doubt going to do for the rest of their lives. Quite a few of them were black.

Since we were his star pupils, Skinny gave us a special task, one which we took to with great enthusiasm. He organized us to perform a minstrel show for the entire school. Only boys would act out the parts on stage, but the girls would do the rest of the work. I don't know where he got the "script," but

minstrel shows were still performed by some civic organizations; maybe he was a member of the Kiwanis Club or some
other do-gooder organization and he got it from there. We
auditioned, were assigned roles, and began to rehearse. One of
our section's science brains, a nice guy but a bit of a sissy, was
chosen to play the straight man or "Interlocuter." The rest of us
were given a variety of stock minstrel roles with standard minstrel names like "Rastus." We rehearsed diligently, learning a
large number of lines. The main idea was that the Interlocutor
would ask each of us questions, and we would answer in our
best imitation of what we thought was southern black speech,
tripping over the words and twisting them around nonsensi-
cally to get a laugh out of the audience. Some of us also did
skits, again with the idea of illustrating the natural stupidity
and childishness of black men.

The minstrel show was a great success; not a single teacher
or administrator criticized it. We were all proud of our budding acting talents. We had enjoyed putting on black face and
dressing in outlandish costumes. Best of all, we had relished
being allowed to talk in front of a large audience the way the
actors on *"Amos and Andy"* talked. We were assured that what
we had done was good when my friend, the "expert," told us
that he had talked to a black girl in our grade, and she had told
him that she had not been offended.

I can say now that I have never done something that has
shamed me more than the minstrel show. I do not remember that it bothered me then, but it has troubled me since.
The grossness of it, the inhumanity of it, the way in which
it degraded not just my black classmates but all black people, the casual way in which Skinny assigned it and we did
it—all of these things make me sick now. The sad thing is the
knowledge that so many of my teachers—people who should
have known better in 1960 than to have allowed this to happen—enjoyed it, committing themselves to the same racism
that filled up the tree limbs with dead black bodies.

White people like to say that things have improved for black men and women. Whites complain that blacks keep bitching and moaning about what happened to them in the past, when what they should be doing is getting on with their lives. It is true that not many people dress up in blackface these days, although it is not unknown in college fraternities. And lynching is no longer a fact of life in the South. There are thousands of black office holders, a significant black middle class, even black billionaires and CEOs. Black styles and black music dominate youth culture. So, why rehash the past?

We don't need to belabour the past. Just look at the present. Four decades after the passage of the landmark Civil Rights Acts (and forty-five years since I graduated from high school), more than half of all prisoners in the United States are black, half of more than two million people. At least 65 percent of all prisoners are black in Maryland, Louisiana, Mississippi, South Carolina, Georgia, Virginia, Alabama, Illinois, New Jersey, North Carolina, and the District of Columbia (96 percent black). Researcher Richard Vogel reports that the lifetime likelihood of going to prison is high for minority males. In the process of "crunching numbers," the Bureau of Justice Statistics (BJS) developed a statistical model to predict the chances of Americans going to prison during their lifetime. Their model predicted that a young black man of sixteen in 1991 had a 28.5 percent chance of spending time in prison during his life. This prediction counts only felony convictions and does not include time spent in local or county jails. When social class differences within the black population are factored in, the prospect of poor black males being incarcerated is probably double this figure—closer to 60 percent. And, if we add the differential jail incarceration rates for blacks, a 75 percent likelihood of going to prison is not an unreasonable estimate.

I could go on and talk about poverty and unemployment rates, life expectancies, infant mortality, access to medical care, and the recent rash of nooses that have appeared on office doors, in trees, and in hate mail, and about the rising hatred of our brown-skinned immigrants. But enough said. How are we to explain these appalling disparities except as consequences of the same racism that killed Emmett Till and encouraged us to put on our minstrel show?

The Invisible Hand

NON-FICTION

Father Armand strode into class, tall and gaunt in his black monk's robe, and filled the board with what looked like an outline. Some of us began to copy what he was writing, furiously scribbling in our new notebooks. Except for the noise made by his chalk, there was silence. We had all heard stories about him. He was brilliant. He was brutally strict. He was heir to a large fortune. We would be lucky to escape his class with a passing grade. When he finished at the board, he turned to face us, lit the first of many cigarettes, and began to tell us what we were in for. My stomach sank. Here was a man who could instill terror with a glance. I don't remember what that first lecture was about, except that he said that we would lose points on our exams for spelling mistakes and we had better come to class prepared. Maybe I did not belong here. Maybe I should have enrolled in one of the state teachers' colleges or just gone to work in the glass factory.

In my high school, we weren't encouraged to go to the best schools, no matter how smart we were. We were pretty much on our own, college and career-wise. The guidance counselors gave us tests to see what we were good at and then recommended that we get this or that job, join the army, go to technical school or, if we were bright, go to nursing school or one of the nearby state colleges. At least I had the sense to ignore their advice. One of my cousins had gone to a small Catholic liberal arts college, and I decided to apply there. My dad helped me fill out the application, and, not only did I get accepted, but I also got a scholarship. This was fortunate because my parents could not have afforded the fairly modest (by today's standards) tuition, room, and board that the school charged. I thought of myself as having done something remarkable, not just going to college, but to one a little out of the ordinary. How naive I was not to know that my economic betters were going to schools that I could not have imagined applying to.

Most of my high school classmates did not go to college. Some took factory jobs, others became secretaries, and a few went into the armed forces. I had no desire to do any of these things, so I was proud to be going to college, the first in my extended family to do so. I wouldn't be stuck in the glass factory like my father; I'd get a good job and make something of myself. If, that is, I worked hard and took advantage of the opportunities opening up to me. I felt heavy pressure to succeed. I wanted to please my parents most of all, and I wanted to show the teachers who had not encouraged me that they had made a mistake. I decided to major in economics. Not because I had any predisposition to do so; I had no idea what economics was. I had chosen it randomly. My father said that the application form required that I declare a major. I asked him to read down the list of majors. He read, "Biology," and I said, "No." The same for chemistry. Then he got to economics, and I said, "That sounds good. Put it down."

So, here I was in Father Armand's class, scared to death, wishing I'd gone a little further down the list of majors. But fear is sometimes a wonderful anodyne. I studied economics like a maniac and was rewarded with an A. Better yet, other students began to regard me as someone with brains. After economics, other subjects seemed easy, and I got As in them as well. And best of all, I did not have to hide my abilities. Here there were many capable people, and they were often admired. I remember a student in a history class, a nerd if ever there was one. The course was called "Renaissance and Reformation." The one thing I remember from it was that there were monks in the Middle Ages selling not only wood from the true cross of Christ but milk from the Virgin Mary's breast; this was grist for the mill of my budding atheism. This student actually conversed with the teacher in Latin. I was bowled over.

Father Armand made his economics majors seem special, a chosen few deemed worthy enough to be instructed by him. So, naturally, we felt special. The other instructor, Father Callistus, had been a student of Armand's and was, so to speak, cut from the same cloth. He was even harder and stricter; he once threw me out of class on an examination day because I had forgotten to wear a tie. On another occasion he smacked me on the head when he caught me trying to help a classmate who got stuck while giving his class presentation. But he told us that he thought of us as his children, and this was said with such sincerity that we would have walked through fire for him. Once we snuck him out of the monastery for a night at the racetrack. He flirted with the waitress at a restaurant and told us we could eat meat even though it was Friday.

The monotony and tyranny of high school had made me rebellious, but college seemed so liberating that there did not appear to be anything to rebel against. I was shocked by the system of hazing to which all freshmen were subjected. We were mercilessly tormented by the upperclassmen (it was an all male school) in a ritual called the "rules." We had to wear beanies and back signs, light cigarettes, carry trays in the cafeteria, and submit to room inspection at six o'clock every morning. The inspections were carried out with ruthlessness; beds were ripped apart and young men humiliated in every possible way. Some of my classmates were what then was characterized as effeminate or sissies, and they came in for special and disgustingly brutal scorn. One poor fellow was literally hounded out of the school. At seven o'clock we were allowed to attend mass and get a reprieve from the harassment. Some of us refused to do this, and were then compelled to go outside and run around the statue of the monk who founded the school. All of this was supposed to bond us as a class, but it only made me miserable. The first free day we had, on Sunday, I begged my father to come and take me off campus. He was nice enough to do this, and we went bowling and out for a good meal.

Unfortunately, however, the hazing did not make me want to fight for its abolition. I joined the rules committee the next year and enjoyed torturing a new class. Eventually I did come to oppose this barbarity, but most students either supported rules or were indifferent to them. Later I would learn that people who are oppressed do not usually rebel. Instead they succumb to the "rules," even acting sometimes as if they were reasonable, or else looking for opportunities to oppress others. A law professor explained this once to a group of first-year students. Torturers are trained by being tortured, in much the same way that marines are taught to kill by being trained brutally. Lawyers are educated for the sometimes brutal behavior that they will have to inflict upon others by being subjected to the cruelties of their first year in law school. Workers hate their bosses, but many of them aspire to become supervisors.

This ugly and repressive initiation was connected to what went on in the classroom. You could be antagonistic to one but enjoy the other. In my second year, I told my mother that I would no longer go to church. My rejection of religion had little to do with an intellectual awakening. I still liked my theology classes. Maybe I was reacting to the hypocritical practices of some of the monks. The president of the college had a mistress, and he was only a more extreme version of a number of others. I wrote a scathing denunciation of the sermon on the mount in one theology class, but this was more to irritate the teacher, a holier than thou "visionary" whom I could not stand. In another class, I said to the teacher, "Now you and I both know that there is nothing in the chalice but wine and nothing in the host but bread, and the sooner the church gets rid of the mumbo-jumbo about these becoming the body and blood of Christ the better." Yet I liked this priest and enjoyed his class. I just thought that religion was stupid. Why waste my time with such an unnecessary thing? Why go to mass when I could sleep late?

It was liberating to reject my faith, especially because it unburdened me of some of the guilt that is the stock and trade of Catholicism. However, the abandonment of religion left a void. If the world did not operate according to God's will, how did it work? Few of my teachers had much to say about this, probably because most of them were practicing Catholics. Courses were disconnected entities, enjoyable in themselves but not offering much in the way of insight. I remember the frequent histrionics of my English teachers more than I remember what they taught me. The literature we read was great, but what did it mean? Similarly, I loved studying about the past, but how did it connect to the present? What did it have to say about the civil rights movement and Vietnam?

The teachers who did teach a coherent theory of the world were the economists, and this fact, along with the professors' strong personalities, attracted me to the subject. Economics had a simple but powerful explanation for the way things were. People were assumed to have unlimited wants for material things, while societies were presumed to have limited means to satisfy these wants. Economics was the science that explained how we went about making the choices necessary to resolve this dilemma.

What was especially attractive about economics was its elegance and its counter-intuitive logic. Human beings were motivated by self-interest, and in the marketplaces of capitalism, selfish buyers and sellers confronted and competed with one another. But this heartless competition did not tear the society apart. Instead, as if guided by an invisible hand, the greed of the buyers and sellers resulted in socially optimal production and distribution. This magnificent outcome could be demonstrated with elegant graphs and proven with mathematics. Unlike the lesser social sciences, economics was a true science, whose mysteries could be grasped only by hard study and sacrifice. Those willing to do the work came to feel superior to those who had not been let in on the secrets of the market. A feeling no doubt similar to that felt by the monks, who were learning the secrets of God himself.

The clear implications of economic theory are that it is good to be selfish and that we get what we deserve. It is not only unnecessary to be kind and generous, it is socially destructive, because such behavior interferes with the invisible hand. What is more, in our economic system, we are, as Milton Friedman, great guru of the market and hero of my favorite instructor, put it, "free to choose." If I am unemployed, it is because I choose to be unemployed. In economic jargon, the gain to be had from not working (enjoying my leisure) outweighed the benefit to be had from working at the going wage rate. If I wanted a job, all I had to do was accept less pay, since selfish employers would naturally offer more jobs at the lower wage. Or I could choose to invest in "human capital" by going to school and making myself productive enough to warrant an employer paying me more money. Finally, if I do not like my job, then I am free to quit. If no one likes a particular job, then employers will have to change it—make it a better job or pay a premium for its undesirable characteristics. In the end, the employers will supply those jobs that employees most desire.

As I became adept at economics, my teachers prepared me for graduate school and a career as a professor. I had already decided that I would become a teacher. I had a knack for it. I was always so well prepared for exams that I had time to tutor others. I conducted seminars for my friends before examinations in the dormitory lounges. Once, when a student outside our little group attended and began to make comments, the others shouted him down. I became Father Callistus's assistant, grading his statistics homework assignments. He also let me teach a few classes, as did Father Armand. These were nerve-wracking experiences, and I made a dreadful error in a statistics class, but I knew that this was what I wanted to do.

Later, when I told my own students that I never worried about getting a job when I was in college, they looked at me as if I were crazy. To most of them, the only point of a college education was to become more employable. I told them that I took whatever courses interested me. The important thing was to "gain ze knowledge," as my Russian French teacher used to say. Luckily, we were still in the great post-Second World War economic boom, and I had every reason to believe that a good job would be waiting for me no matter what I studied. I went to graduate school not so much because of the job it would get me, but because I wanted to continue to study.

Graduate school was not a happy experience. I was immersed in economics and I did well. But most of the other students were too conservative for me. They had already begun to think like economists, whereas I had begun to notice discrepancies between what we were learning and the world around me. They loved to sit around and discuss the workings of the invisible hand, but didn't seem to care that their government was making a wasteland out of Southeast Asia and sending my high school friends off to be slaughtered. I kept asking my labour economics instructor when we were going to study labour unions. When we finally did, and after he had grilled me through three consecutive three-hour seminars, he wondered aloud, "What do the unions want?" Collective action does not accord very well with the economists' belief that what motivates all persons is self-interest.

During my second year, the draft board decided that I belonged in the army. At first, I just accepted the fact of being drafted and probably sent to Vietnam. After more than a year of hassles, I managed to get a teaching job and avoid the draft. I began to teach my own students about the invisible hand.

Economics teaches us that we choose our own path in life by the self-interested or "maximizing" decisions that we make. Little notice is taken of the different facts of life surrounding each person's choices or of the random events that impinge upon them. I did not want to go to Vietnam, and I had no say in the government's decision to wage war there. I was in no way responsible for the decision of the University to deny me and other students fighting against the draft access to its battery of high-powered lawyers. The entire connection between the universities and the government affected me, but I had to take this as a given when I made my choices. Suppose I had been drafted, sent to Vietnam, and killed. Would my parents have been able to console themselves in the knowledge that life was simply a matter of choices?

The Demonstration

FICTION

D anny was sitting in the park with friends. They had been driving around in his parents' car, smoking dope and listening to music. He had gotten so high that on a back road in the state park where he had worked just two years before, he had forgotten where he was. A Creedence Clearwater song had put him on automatic pilot, and when he suddenly snapped back to reality he realized that he was near the campground he used to police late at night.

They were talking about the war in that slow, disconnected, marijuana speech. Dope and the war were tied together in his mind. He got high for the first time in Pittsburgh when he was in graduate school. Some high school buddies lived close to his rooming house, and he spent his free time at their apartment. The place was a magnet for kids from his hometown, and guys back from Vietnam used to crash there. They'd come home emotionally damaged, and it wasn't long before their baffled parents were glad to see them away from home again. They gravitated to the city, where the sixties were in full swing. They brought their drugs with them. Marijuana, hashish, LSD, opium—they were walking pharmacies. The vets who were Danny's age had gone to Vietnam in 1964 and '65.

They still favoured alcohol; the druggies called them "juicers." Those a few years younger used drugs—any and all drugs, anything they could get. All of them were fucked up. All the time. Two of his high school classmates used to drive around the back streets of Pittsburgh late at night shooting out streetlights and storefronts. They went to a party at the apartment of a girl he liked and stole everything in sight. The younger guys could be just as violent. Jerry was a marine, so brutalized by the war that he had lost his mind. One night he and Danny were having a beer in the old Liberty Tavern. Jerry said that another vet from a town up the river a few miles had some good dope, but he wouldn't sell any of it to him. Matter of factly, Jerry said, "Let's go kill him." He wasn't kidding, and Danny had to talk him out of it. When Jerry returned to Vietnam, he wrote Danny a letter begging for some LSD. A year later, he was in prison after ramming a police car in Mississippi on his way to Mardi Gras. He escaped and was last heard to be living somewhere in the San Juan Islands in Washington.

Danny thought that marijuana was the best thing going. That first time he had smoked it, it was some dope from Vietnam laced with opium, provided by the guy Jerry had wanted to kill. After a few minutes he felt flushed and disoriented. Everything seemed to have a new importance, a depth he was seeing for the first time. The music from the stereo slowed down, and the Motown music he usually hated sounded good. "People say I'm the life of the party, cause I tell a joke or two" cascaded from the speakers with raw emotions he hadn't noticed before. His friends' voices came at him from a distance, but the feeling he usually had that they were keeping something from him, that they were privy to secrets he could only guess at, disappeared and he felt for the first time that he fit in, that he knew the secrets too. When the juicers visited, he had some special knowledge they didn't. It was a great feeling to turn one of them on. That evening, really ripped, he started seeing cartoon characters when he closed his eyes. Donald Duck, Uncle Scrooge, Bugs Bunny. He couldn't stop laughing. As he got used to the drug, he found that he could speak with a profundity he didn't know he possessed. Conversations would run late into the night, usually ending at a nearby restaurant where they'd all have an early breakfast. Then he'd crash on the living room couch and miss his university classes.

He had graduated from college in 1967 and moved to the city to attend graduate school. All he did the first year was study, day and night sitting at the desk in his rooming house quarters, watching the traffic on the busy street below. The day Lyndon Johnson announced he would not seek re-election, he went out and got drunk and almost fought with a serviceman he argued with in a bar. In early October he had walked around the corner to Chief's Bar at noon to watch a World Series game. He had planned to have lunch there, drink a couple beers, and go back to study. But a big red-headed black man, nicknamed Red, who drove a jitney cab, stopped in for a quick drink. He ordered a triple shot of vodka, put his arm around Danny, and said to the Chief, "And give my friend one too." Chief poured out two large glasses, and Red said, "Cheers." Danny had no choice but to gulp down the cheap and lethal liquid and say, "Thanks." Red then left, and Danny ordered lunch. But the damage was done. He had a beer every inning, went home, and threw up. He seldom drank hard liquor after that.

Danny didn't fit in very well in graduate school. The students were aggressively competitive, and the teachers odd and disorienting. He thought that inside his arid classrooms you'd never know there was a war raging, boys from his hometown were being shot at, and here in this conservative blue-collar city, protests against the war were escalating. He had enjoyed economics in college, but a steady diet of production functions, Slutsky's equation, revealed preferences, turnpike theorems, and the like had his head spinning and thinking about the disconnect between all the abstraction and the real world outside the seminar rooms. Luckily, he didn't have much time to think. Too many books to read, articles to copy, mathematics to learn. He had taken a calculus class his senior year, but the calculus used in his first graduate economics course sent him to the library to get books from which he could teach himself the rudiments of partial derivatives and differentiation. His landlady roamed around at night telling her lodgers, "Study, study, boys." And that's what he did, taking a break for a long walk in the city on Sundays.

The one thing that broke the academic monotony was the Friday afternoon seminar. The department invited a noted scholar to give a talk every Friday at 3:30. These were invariably uninteresting and usually provided a forum for faculty members to drone on about their pet ideas. Was the money supply endogenous or exogenous? Was capital putty or clay? Attendance was mandatory, so to prepare for the torture, Danny and some friends went to a nearby bar about two o'clock and drank as much as they could, stumbling into the seminar room just in time for the department chairman to make the introductions. The only problem was that you would have to make a conspicuous exit if you had to empty your bladder.

Danny shocked himself by getting all As. Even in econometrics, where he had been lost from the first class. Much of his confusion was due to the ineptitude of the instructor, who was so awful that his graduate assistant pushed him aside during one lecture and taught the class himself. They all walked out in protest after one particularly atrocious performance. How he attained an A was a mystery until much later when he had a conversation with the graduate assistant. This young man was distraught that he had received a B; how would he get a good job after graduation with poor marks on his record? He asked Danny what grade he had gotten, and nearly collapsed when Danny told him. About a month later it struck Danny what had happened. The assistant's last name was Bates. Danny's was Gates. The professor had given them each other's grade.

Flushed with his success, Danny happily anticipated the new term. But for better or worse, 1968 brought his graduate career to a halt. First came the drugs. Some of his pals from home moved to the city. And the vets started coming back with their dope. Before the term was half over, he was getting high every night and sometimes during the day as well. He had an interesting teacher, a man in his early thirties, who wore his hair long under a headband and dressed in jeans and black T-shirts. He was a well-known antiwar activist; he and some accomplices had locked the chancellor of the university in an elevator in protest against his avid support for the war and career as a CIA operative. Along with a larger group, this teacher had invaded an exclusive private club during a dinner honoring the city's business elite. The protesters were spit upon by the diners.

One day, Dr. Austen spent an entire class talking about the war in Vietnam. Danny's classmates were enraged by this. They had examinations to pass and comprehensives to prepare for and their professor was wasting their time propagandizing against the war, violating the scientific objectivity he was supposed to uphold. A few of the more strident complainers said that Dr. Austen was high on drugs. Danny doubted that the teacher was high, but Danny was. He wanted to be high for as many everyday events as possible: driving a car, riding a bus, going to a concert, watching television in a bar, eating in a restaurant. It was like living life all over again, experiencing things like a child, for the first time. Marijuana had so unleashed his inhibitions that he got high in an empty third-floor classroom of the Depression-era skyscraper that housed most of the university's classrooms and administrative offices. Then he'd go to Dr. Austen's class, nodding knowingly at whatever the professor said. The day of the Vietnam lecture, he nodded nonstop. After class, he went to a local bookstore and bought some books and magazines with materials about Vietnam and the war. He decided that there was more to education than graduate economics. The next week he participated in his first demonstration.

It would have been fine to continue this new life. Get high, study, read, protest the war, listen to Bob Dylan, the Beatles, Grateful Dead, Mothers of Invention. He smoked a few joints with a girl he knew, dressed up in bellbottoms and a peace sign chain, and went to a concert. For three hours they were entranced by Jerry Garcia, Lou Reed, the Velvet Underground, and the Fugs. Danny imagined that everyone there was high and happy. He was, and all the more so afterward when the girl dragged him off to bed. It was great to be alive and young in 1968. Exactly one week later, he got a letter from his local draft board. He was wanted elsewhere.

There is nothing like a draft notice to concentrate a person's hatred of an unpopular war. He had been opposed to the Vietnam War since his sophomore year in college when he heard a man speak who had burned his draft card. He had gone into the talk hostile to the speaker but came away admiring him. Then friends started coming back with harrowing stories of violence. A black guy Danny knew, a marine, told him that he was in a firefight somewhere in the countryside. A young girl ran across a field below him. His sergeant had ordered him to shoot her. He refused; nothing happened to him. Such was the breakdown of command and the fear among officers and platoon leaders that they might be "fragged." Not one returning soldier supported the war. They were ashamed that they had ever been gung-ho for combat. Once Danny had begun to read about the war and the Vietnamese, he started to hope that the United States would be defeated. His admiration for the Vietnamese people and for the National Liberation Front and Ho Chi Minh grew and deepened.

The problem was Danny's family. His parents were typical small-town patriots. His father had been in the South Pacific in the Second World War, and as he had gotten older, he had become rigid in his views. He had voted for Goldwater, a deranged thing to do as far as Danny was concerned. They had had an argument, and his dad accused him of not respecting the flag. His mother was always concerned with what people would say if you did anything out of the ordinary. His grandfather was the most conservative of the lot; he bragged that he had voted against Franklin Roosevelt all four times. Danny couldn't imagine telling any of them that he was going to refuse to be inducted, or move to Canada.

For the next few months, he engaged in a war of attrition with the draft board. He appealed his reclassification. It was turned down. He then took the draft physical at the induction centre in the city's downtown. As soon as he got up he started smoking cigarettes and drinking coffee, hoping that his blood pressure would rise enough to disqualify him for service. He knew this was a longshot; an army doctor hadn't noticed that a friend of his had one eye. The sergeant who herded the potential inductees around acted as if they were already in the army, cajoling and threatening them. During his physical examination, Danny made sure to tell the doctors that there was a history of tuberculosis in his family. He acted like Mr. McGoo for the eye technician. On the mental aptitude tests, he chose answers that might mark him as poor soldier material. Would he rather read poetry or go hunting? Poetry, of course.

Nothing worked, and he was inducted. He was to go to Fort Jackson, South Carolina, for boot camp. He caught a break from the draft board, one of whose members was a good friend of his grandfather and a former customer when Danny had been a paperboy. He would be allowed to finish the current semester before he had to go. He was happy to have some extra time, but every day his panic level rose. He went to see his radical professor. Dr. Austen told him that he should talk to a biology teacher who was acting as an informal draft counselor. He rushed over to the biology department and met

Dr. Stanley, a blunt and sharp-tongued man of about thirty. He told Danny that he didn't have time for anyone who hadn't made a commitment to refuse military service. Ordinarily Danny would have thanked him and left but, probably out of desperation, he stayed and argued his case. Dr. Stanley finally softened and recommended that Danny see a lawyer and try to file a class action lawsuit on behalf of all graduate students, arguing that the termination of their student deferments was both illegal and not in the public interest.

Danny barely remembered the next few weeks. He met the lawyer, and they filed the lawsuit. To save money, Danny typed the brief himself. The local draft board responded by reclassifying him I-A, essentially rolling back the clock to the day before he got his draft notice. They then drafted him a second time. He appealed again and lost, but the board let him finish another term. He got another letter ordering him to report to Fort Jackson, this time in September. He was running out of options. Either go or get out of the country. He went to see his academic advisor to tell him he wouldn't be back for a third year of studies. His advisor was opposed to the war, too, but he was a not a radical. He said to Danny, "Why don't you try to get a teaching job. You could get a deferment that way."

Danny said, "But I don't even have a master's degree; how could I get a job?"

Dr. Chadwick said, "Well, what harm can come from trying? I'll let you know if I hear of any openings." Three weeks later, Dr. Chadwick motioned him aside after class and told him that one of the university's branch campuses, about one hundred miles away, had an opening for an economics teacher. Another student in the department was set to accept it but turned it down when he got a better offer. It was now early August. The fall term began in three weeks, and they were desperate. Their only economics professor had just retired, and they had no one to teach the four classes already fully subscribed with students. Dr. Chadwick gave him the name and phone number of the college's dean and told him to call right away.

Danny ran to his rooming house and, after getting as much change as he could find in his room, called the dean on the pay phone in the hallway. The dean was at lunch, so he nervously walked around the block for an hour and called back. He got the dean, told a few lies about his training, and set up an interview for the next week. The directions the dean gave him for getting to campus were so long and involved that he ran out of space on the notebook page he was using and had to write the rest of them on the wall above the phone. He drove to his parents' house that weekend and begged them to buy him a sports coat and a good pair of pants and shoes for the interview. Despite their misgivings about his rapidly changing politics, Danny sensed that they didn't want him to go to Vietnam. They wished him luck and let him use their car for the drive to the college.

The route to the campus from Danny's hometown was different than the one from the city. Danny got lost a few miles from his destination and managed to arrive for his two o'clock interview at 1:58. The dean immediately remarked on Danny's long hair and sideburns. They made small talk, but the dean soon got down to business. There would be four classes to teach, each one a separate preparation and each with an enrollment of about forty. If classes got larger, they could be split into two sections and an overload payment made. Could Danny teach statistics? "Yes," he said without hesitation, right away thinking that he was not at all qualified to do so. Could he teach this? "Yes." Could he teach that? "Yes." He would have said he could teach modern dance to get this job. After the dean told him some things about the college, mainly that drug and alcohol use weren't tolerated and that he (the dean) often filled in for sick faculty, he gave Danny over to another administrator who took him on a short tour of campus.

The college didn't appear to be much of a place. The physical setting was pretty; the college sat on six hundred acres of woodland donated, he was told, by a local coal company. There were only a few buildings: two classroom and administrative halls, a student union, and four or five dormitories, but they were all made of an attractive stone that gave them the appearance of ski lodges. The tour was so brief that the beauty of the place was lost on him. At the time he didn't even think about the fact that he had not been given a meal or travel reimbursement. He was allotted a small Coke in the student union and was grateful for that. The dean's aide had something to do with the dormitories, and he hinted that Danny might be able to get a job as a dormitory counsellor, which would provide him with free room and board.

Things went down to the wire. Danny got a letter from the college president on August 28, one week before he was to go to Fort Jackson. His salary was a pathetic $7,200, barely more than he made working summers at the factory, but they threw in the dorm job. He told the draft board right away, and they said they'd reconsider his classification. Before he had a chance to start worrying about teaching four wildly different courses, commuting to the university for a class, and living in a dorm at a college in the middle of nowhere, he went out and got high.

The change in Danny's life was dramatic, but he was usually too tired and happy not to be in the army to notice. Except for the classes he had taught as an undergraduate, he had no experience, and now he had four different courses to teach. The classes met in time slots which ranged in length from 50 to 150 minutes, and he was expected to talk knowledgeably during those minutes. He had to prepare the equivalent of twelve lectures per week for fifteen weeks each semester. In one semester this meant that he had to assemble at least 148 lectures, assuming that he gave three tests in each of the four courses. He wrote these lectures out in longhand, and each lecture required approximately seven pages of legal-size paper. This yielded a total of 1036 pages of lectures per term. He worked on lectures, morning, noon, and night, seven days a week.

In 1969 there was no escaping the larger world. The war raged on, and Danny's study of it deepened. It soon struck him that the new political views he was embracing made him question everything he had learned, and he began to see his new workplace in political terms. He was fired from the job as dorm assistant within four months, because he refused to search students' rooms for drugs on weekends when they were away from the college. Neither the dean, who turned out to be a pompous ass—he said to students that he did not stand on formalities; they could call him "Doctor" instead of "Dean"— nor the housing director saw anything wrong with this blatant violation of civil liberties. It was his first taste of employer morality. He learned that the president of the school, who lacked a PhD though he insisted on being addressed as "doctor," had purchased property adjacent to the school before the campus had been constructed, knowing that as the college grew, the property's value would too.

He tried to get his colleagues riled up about Vietnam but without much success. They either supported the war or were too provincial to think about it. Much the same was true for the students, although for them the war was too close to ignore. To his surprise, a Spanish teacher and the editor of the student newspaper organized an anti-war "read-in" during the first national anti-war mobilization that fall. Danny's war veteran students were upset that he cancelled class in support of the national protest, and he noted with dismay that he was the only teacher who did.

The highlights of the protest were a recitation of the names of the U.S. soldiers killed in the war and a reading of anti-war poetry by the Spanish instructor. Some of the poems were in Spanish, so the teacher had handed out mimeographed pages with the translations. Danny and the others were sitting on benches underneath the flagpole, a tiny knot of students and faculty. He was moved by the reading of the names and the poems; he grieved for the families and especially for the suffering of the Vietnamese. He wished with all his heart that they would defeat the United States as they had the French. He hated everyone responsible for the war, and he hoped that Johnson, Westmoreland, and all the other war criminals would die horrible deaths. He yearned for the courage to run the Vietcong flag up the pole. He hardly noticed that a group of students, some of them his own and all of them veterans, were approaching the group. They rushed in, grabbed the poetry translations from the protestors' hands, and ripped them up. Then just as suddenly they were gone.

In the weeks before the school protest, Danny had visited his old friends in the city and in his hometown. At a party, his friend Paul said, "Why don't we have a demonstration in the park back home. We'll get all the vets to come. Maybe they'll throw away their medals. We'll get loudspeakers and a tape player. Have Phil Ochs' 'White Boots Marching in a Yellow Land' playing. Invite the high school kids. Man, everyone in town will freak out. This will blow the pigs' minds. Danny, you can be the main speaker."

Danny was saying "cool" to everything Paul said until the last sentence. Danny be the main speaker? In the park where he used to wait for his father to come through the glass factory tunnel after work? His name would be in the newspaper; no way he could hide this from his family. But there was also no way he could refuse. He was a college teacher, and his speech would be legitimized because of this. No one could say, "Well, this is just a prank by a bunch of drug addicts." He could say what the veterans might not be able to say, and this would make their testimony more powerful. He agreed to do it, and he, Paul, and some others began that night to make preparations. They set the date as the Saturday after the national mobilization. People were given assignments—getting a permit from the town, getting the sound equipment, lining up the vets, having food and drinks available, putting a notice in the local paper, making fliers, contacting high school protesters—and their excitement grew as the night gave way to morning.

Whenever Danny faced a decision, he tried to visualize what would happen if he did something and if he did not. The main decision was whether he should tell his parents about this. He foresaw a shocked reaction. His father wouldn't say much; he never did. But his mother would. She wouldn't be able to imagine facing her neighbors and relatives. It was all right to try to get a job and avoid the draft—in secret—but it was not all right to make common cause with hippies and draft card burners. So, he thought about not telling them. What would happen? A lot of hand wringing and then it would blow over. But maybe he should tell them. He was an adult. Why not just let them know he was doing it? Why sneak around like a child?

He wasn't prepared for his mother's wailing when he told her. She used all her tricks to talk him out of it. "Oh, Danny, you can't do that. Danny, why would you do that? You know what those guys you hang out with are like. They won't show up. They're just using you. Why would a college teacher lower himself to be part of that gang? You'll get arrested, then what? You might lose your job. And your deferment." It wasn't so much the words but her tone that bothered him. That tone that said that after all she had done for him, how could he do this to her. That tone that played on the guilty feelings rooted in his being. That tone that spoke of her (and his) fear of authority, of losing respectability, of being someone different. He argued with her, got angry, and hung up. But he knew he wouldn't go to the demonstration. He spent hours thinking about it. He tried to rationalize it. His mother was probably right. Most of his friends were more interested in drugs than politics. They probably wouldn't have gotten things organized well enough. No one would have shown up anyway.

And so there it was. He didn't speak at the rally because he didn't want to embarrass his mother. He made some lame excuse and stayed away. It was a turning point in his life. He rarely saw anyone from his hometown after that. They went their separate ways. He eventually did develop some courage, and he never let his parents' voices still his conscience. Still, damage was done.

Later, when he thought about his decision, he saw that the system did a lot more than wage war on a nation of peasants. Just like rich countries had colonized poor ones, so too did the entire oppressive beast—through constant propaganda drummed into your head by newspapers, churches, schools, and, worst of all, by your own parents—colonize your mind. As you tried to make changes, you had to change yourself as well.

Taking the Pledge

NON-FICTION

In 1991, nearly thirty years after I had graduated from high school, my twin sons, then twelve years old and seventh graders at a Pittsburgh public school, read a story in their language arts class. A young teacher, admired and respected by her students, refused to stand for the pledge of allegiance to the flag. For this act of conscience she was fired by the local school board. She filed suit, charging a violation of her First Amendment right of free speech. The court ordered her reinstatement, but in the end she decided not to return to her old job. After reading the story, the class discussed it with their teacher. He was of the view that it was wrong for the teacher not to stand because this was disrespectful to the beliefs of others. One of my sons agreed with the teacher in the story, arguing that no one should have to stand. Besides, he said, there was not "liberty and justice for all" in the United States, so the pledge was a lie. My son's comments were met with stern criticism from his teacher who quickly shut off further discussion.

A few days later, my wife and I met with our son's team of teachers. We mentioned the flag salute story to the language arts teacher and expressed our disappointment with his reaction to it. Wouldn't this have been an opportunity to strengthen the students' understanding of the importance of free speech in a democracy? The teacher, bearded and casually dressed, tried to disarm us. He was a product of the sixties, he said, and did not personally care if the students said the pledge. But out of respect for the beliefs of others, the students had to stand. My wife disagreed. She said that standing was the same thing as saying the words. She told him that our son had, in fact, been refusing to stand for the pledge in his homeroom and that we had sent the required note to the school stating that we did not object to his actions. The teacher said that this would be unacceptable in his homeroom; had our son been his charge, he would have had to stand in the hall during the pledge. My wife told him that if that had happened, the teacher would have faced a lawsuit, at which point the conversation ended.

For two weeks our son sat quietly at his desk during the pledge. Then we received a phone call from his teacher-team leader who left a message for us to contact her about a problem with our son. We could not reach her that day, and she did not return our calls. We worried about what our son had done. When he came home, he told us that his team leader was angry that he would not stand for the pledge. She had walked by his homeroom, seen that he was not standing, marched in, and confronted him. When he refused to stand, she grabbed him by the arm and pulled him out of the room. I was so incensed that I ranted for three days, but we let it go because she did not do it again. Then, she called a second time. Could I speak with my son about his refusal to stand? He was setting a bad example for the other students. I asked her if maybe my son wasn't setting a good example by showing his classmates that we live in a free country. I told her that one of the reasons we sent our children to the urban public schools was so that they would get to know and understand classmates of different races, religions, and beliefs. If the teachers themselves did not respect differences among their students, then weren't we all in trouble? Finally, I reminded her that my son could not be legally required to stand for the pledge. In a distant voice, she said, Okay, she'd let it drop. I said goodbye, and she said, "Have a nice day."

Our other son, then fifteen, was a sophomore in a city high school. He wouldn't stand for the pledge either, and he too was hassled by his teachers. During his freshman year, his homeroom teacher insisted that he stand and, when he refused, we got a phone call. After some discussion, his teacher said that we would have to write a letter giving our approval for our son's behavior. We refused to do this; our son continued to sit, and nothing happened. Until, that is, a substitute teacher confronted him and publicly berated him for insulting his country. Didn't he realize that the city's taxpayers were paying for his education? He told her that he had a job and paid taxes, too. She persisted. Why wouldn't he stand? He just didn't want to. Eventually, he explained that he had moral reasons for not standing, and she gave up. But during the next year, this substitute became his regular homeroom teacher, and we went through another round. This time she pulled out all the stops to pressure us to get him to stand. She kept asking if he had a religious reason for not standing, implying that this would be acceptable. We told her that his reasons were moral, but she did not appear able to grasp this. Finally, she aimed her big gun by hinting that other students were harassing him, and there was a chance that he would be physically harmed. We advised her that she had better see to it that this did not happen, perhaps by explaining to the class that no one had to stand for the pledge. Our fears were allayed when our son told us that he had never been threatened and what the teacher really feared was that other students would refuse to stand.

We wasted a lot of energy trying to uphold our sons' right to peacefully refuse to salute a flag in a public school classroom. We were surprised by the persistence of the teachers, and amazed and saddened by the ironies that abounded here.

Our younger son's antagonist was a black woman teaching in a school that had an overwhelmingly black student body. Their parents were, for the most part, poor, and they lived in neighborhoods ravaged by underemployment, substandard housing, drugs, gangs, and the highest rates of infant mortality in the nation. They faced the same brutal discrimination faced by all black persons, and their prospects were bleak. Was it too much to expect her to have seen the hypocrisy of the pledge of allegiance with its propaganda of "liberty and justice for all"? How could any black person believe this, let alone pledge allegiance to it?

All of the teacher-patriots were members of the powerful Pittsburgh Federation of Teachers. Through aggressive organizing and bargaining, punctuated in the early years by long strikes and defiance of court injunctions, this union had won contracts that were the envy of teachers across the state. City teachers were among the highest paid wage earners in the area; salaries in excess of $60,000 per year were common. An excellent grievance procedure and system of local union stewards had practically eliminated the power of the School Board and the administration to arbitrarily discipline teachers. In other words, the union had secured the civil liberties of its members, their right to act as independent, self-respecting professionals. One would think, therefore, that the teachers would appreciate the importance of civil liberties. Yet this was not the case. It was fine for the teachers to stand up to their employers and demand that their rights be respected. Yet, let a student demand the same and the teachers became as authoritarian as the steel moguls who once made their parents beg for their supper.

So, what was going on here? Why, in situations that must have been common knowledge in the two schools, did not a single teacher offer my sons support? Why had seemingly liberal and progressive instructors, loyal union members all, made such an issue out of what was essentially a mindless act of obedience to the state?

Several explanations might be offered. When teachers do things that students do not like, the teachers often try to pass the blame along to the administration. It is hard to see, however, how administrators could have punished a teacher whose students exercised their legal right not to salute the flag. If a teacher had been disciplined, the union would surely have filed and won a grievance. A second excuse might be that parents would cause trouble if they found out that students refused to say the pledge. Other students besides my sons had refused to stand, but after receiving a call from a teacher, their parents ordered them to stand, and they did. Teachers might have faced some parental anger, but teachers did not mind angry parents when they struck to benefit themselves. Besides, parents cannot do much to teachers so strongly protected by union contract. And, in any case, is it not the job of teachers to challenge their students to think critically about all issues, to be leaders who develop new ideas rather than just followers of old ones? If teachers never step outside conventional beliefs, they might not face parental antagonisms, but they also will not help their students to develop the imaginations necessary to live fulfilling lives.

Another possible explanation might be that the teachers were, themselves, unaware of or unwilling to exercise their duty to promote critical thinking. As a college teacher for most of my adult life, I can attest to the worthlessness of much of what passes for teacher education. Somehow it is imagined that a student who does not major in an academic discipline will know enough about a subject to teach it to others. The ignorance of education majors is legendary, yet they all manage to get As in their education classes. The person who taught my sons history or economics may never have taken an advanced course in these fields. Public school teachers are unlikely to have had a critical education or to have mastered a subject area, so it is little wonder that they might be incapable of making a critical analysis or instilling in their students the importance of civil liberties.

Still, blaming the teachers begs a question: why are teachers so often lacking in critical intelligence? Why are they "trained" in such a thoughtless manner? If, as our leaders keep telling us, our young people are inadequately educated, then why do our schools tread along the same tired paths? The time wasted trying to make my sons conform could have been spent teaching them to think for themselves.

To know why teachers expended such extraordinary effort to get my children to salute the flag, we have to ask what it is that schools are all about. In my view, schools are essentially purveyors of misinformation and promoters of behavior consistent with the requirements of the economic system. Most students are going to be workers someday. They will be expected to work hard at jobs requiring limited skills and to obey orders. Political and business leaders argue that the education system is failing because it is not producing people literate enough to do the work that will help the United States compete with our economic rivals. But this is largely propaganda, which we can see clearly when these same critics also propose a return to the "basics" and renewed emphasis on discipline, the very things least likely to produce an educated citizenry. The truth is that the number of jobs requiring extensive technical, scientific, or literary skills is shrinking as a percentage of total employment. Our schools have always produced enough workers to fill these slots, and if they do not today, it is because the good students now want to make as much money as they can with as little effort as possible. Is there a shortage of lawyers or bond brokers or accountants? Would none of these people have been capable of becoming scientists or engineers?

No, what the schools are expected to do is churn out people who will do what they are told and not expect too much in return. What business leaders want is people who will work harder for less money and keep their mouths shut. They do not want liberally educated, critical thinkers, precisely because such people will ask questions and insist on their rights. It is one thing to get a few future lawyers to become scientists instead, but it is quite another to encourage people to develop themselves as fully as possible.

Flag saluting and the nationalism of which it is a vital part are perfect vehicles to produce the docile persons that the system needs. They teach that obedience is more important than thinking. Someday, students will have to obey their employers. Someday, they will have to march off to war. What better way to get them ready than to make them pray to the flag every day?

When we examine the so-called education crisis with a critical eye, we see that the schools have not failed. They are doing what they have always done, preparing people for a lifetime of thoughtless work and consumption. During the first Gulf War, principals gave teachers yellow ribbons to pass out to their classes. The teachers did it. The students wore them and wrote letters to the troops. Critical thinking, much less opposition, were virtually nonexistent. If actual death and destruction cannot elicit thought, economic warfare won't either.

There is a disaster in the public schools, but it has little to do with the inability of our students to read and write. Our education crisis is a reflection of a deepening social malaise. Our society has become more polarized, with a small stratum of wealthy people confronting a mass of wealthless people facing grim futures. The poor, largely minority, students in our urban schools have little to look forward to; there is not and will not be meaningful work for them to do.

Teachers face sullen and unhappy young people, products of severe social dysfunction, and instead of trying to liberate them, they make them salute flags. This is not likely to work, so they will turn the screws tighter. The schools will become more prison-like. After all, more black men of college age are in prison than in college. It is an insidious system and likely to become more so.

ADDENDUM

Since this essay was published, the public schools of the United States, under mandates put forward in George W. Bush's "No Child Left Behind" program, have become·still more regimented. Consider the following quotation from an article by two prominent education scholars:

"Today, urban schools are adroitly organized around the same principles as factory production lines. According to [Jonathan] Kozol rising test scores, social promotion, outcome-based objectives, time management, success for all, authentic writing, accountable talk, active listening, and zero noise constitute part of the dominant discourse in public schools. Most urban public schools have adopted business and market work related themes and managerial concepts that have become part of the vocabulary used in classroom lessons and instruction. In the market-driven classrooms, students negotiate, sign contracts, and take ownership of their own learning. In many classrooms, students can volunteer as the pencil manager, soap manager, door manager, line manager, time manager, and coatroom manager. In some fourth-grade classrooms, teachers record student assignments and homework using earning charts. In these schools, teachers are referred to as classroom managers, principals are identified as building managers, and students are viewed as learning managers. It is commonplace to view schoolchildren as assets, investment, productive units, or team players. Schools identify the skills and knowledge that students need to learn and acquire as commodities and the products to be consumed in the educational marketplace. Under the current climate of the No Child Left Behind school reform movement, teachers are regarded as efficiency technicians and encouraged to use strict Skinnerian control methods and techniques to manage and teach students in their classroom. Kozol writes that in the market-driven model of public education, teachers are viewed

as floor managers in public schools, whose job it is to pump
some added-value into undervalued children."

Note: The quote at the end of "Minstrel Show" is from Richard Vogel,
"Capitalism and Incarceration Revisited," *Monthly Review*, Sept. 2003.
The quote at the end of "Taking the Pledge" is from Peter McLaren
and Ramin Farahmandpur, "The Pedagogy of Oppression," *Monthly
Review*, July/August 2006.

III.
The Workaday World

Revelation

NON-FICTION

Legal pad in hand, I strode into the room, trying to look confident. Forty mostly young faces watched me, probably wondering how heavy the workload would be and how easy the grading. I lit a cigarette and passed out a stack of note cards. In those days you could smoke, and I burned up three or four Lucky Strikes or Old Golds each fifty-minute class. I told the students to place their names, addresses, and phone numbers on the cards, as well as the reasons they were taking this course. I'd had teachers who had done this, so I thought it would be an appropriate thing to do. Plus it took a few minutes, as did my description of the course and explanation of the requirements. Fifty minutes is an eternity to a new instructor, and I had already begun to tremble at the thought of a 150-minute night class. Unfortunately, introductions, including a roll call, took only fifteen minutes, so I had to start teaching.

Looking up at the ceiling I said, "Economics is the study of how societies allocate their resources to satisfy the unlimited wants that people have for goods and services in the face of the limited means that societies have to satisfy these wants." I began to explain this in terms of the "production possibilities curve" illustrated in the textbook, a five-hundred-page tome used in schools where the more sophisticated and famous textbook of Paul Samuelson might have been too difficult. A few weeks later, I would walk into my office to find another teacher and a student huddled over my copy of Samuelson, which they had retrieved from my bookshelf. This teacher, an old windbag who taught speech and believed that all a person needed for success was enthusiasm, was excoriating me for Samuelson's alleged communism. I told them both to get the hell out of my office.

The production curve showed that a country could not have whatever output it wanted, because it did not have unlimited resources. Therefore tradeoffs had to be made; on the graph the tradeoff was between guns and butter. As I turned from the blackboard, on which I had drawn the curve, I started to explain why it was concave to the origin. Inadvertently I looked directly at the students. Their faces were dumb with incomprehension and boredom. In a panic I drew out one of the index cards from the pile on the desk. "Mr. Miller, can you tell us why the curve slopes downward and to the right?" Mr. Miller looked up at me with wide eyes and shrugged his shoulders. "Got me," he answered. The class tittered, and, mortified, I answered the question myself. It would be more than ten years before I called on someone directly by name again. And I ditched the index cards.

The course continued in an unsatisfactory manner for a few more weeks, me droning on about supply and demand and the kids' eyes glazing over. I was so disgusted after one class that I went to the library to read *Sports Illustrated*. As I was glancing at the rack of magazines, I noticed one containing an article about the economy. I picked up the journal, a small, booklet-sized periodical called *Monthly Review*. It was described on the cover as an "independent socialist magazine." I wondered how it had managed to get into our library, whose librarian would not allow students to sign out certain books.

The article was interesting, so I read the whole issue. Then I went into the stacks and started reading back issues. The writing was clear and insightful and like nothing I had ever read in economics. Later I returned looking for similar periodicals, and I happened upon *Ramparts* and *The Nation*. I was so impressed that I took out subscriptions. Writers I had never heard of—Paul Sweezy, Harry Magdoff, Carey McWilliams, Noam Chomsky—were providing me with new insights into the workings of our economic system or, as these scholars called it, "our political economy."

Armed with this new material, I walked into class around the middle of the term, started to lecture on the week's topic, and then suddenly threw my notes onto the floor and slammed the textbook down on the desk. I declared that we were going to talk about something more interesting and relevant. With that I launched into a discussion of the war in Vietnam, the inequality of wealth and income, and the economic disparities between blacks and whites. A lively give-and-take followed, my first experience with teaching as it should be done. During the remainder of the term, we covered most of the traditional topics, but we also spent time debating the issues of the day. I began to stake out my territory as a radical, someone with unorthodox ideas who was not afraid to express them. I knew that not all students would like my new approach. Some of them, like the ex-marine who said that he wanted to strangle me after one particularly outrageous class, would hate me. But most would rather be challenged than bored, and I would rather be provocative than boring.

Two Campaigns

NON-FICTION

College teachers think they are the most important persons on campus; after all, they teach the students and get special titles and deference. However, like all modern workplaces, a college functions as the result of the coordinated activities of all the workers. Teachers tend to respect and interact with those who stand above them in the workplace hierarchy: department heads, deans, presidents, and board members. Those below — the secretaries, custodians, clerical staff, food-service workers, and maintenance people — most professors either ignore or treat as servants. Teachers expect these workers to understand that they are "professors" and deserving of automatic respect and indulgence. When this is not forthcoming, tempers flare and ugly incidents occur. I have seen teachers berate secretaries and janitors publicly, something they would never do to those in authority. Such behavior breeds resentment and makes it nearly impossible for the college's workers to form a united front against the employer.

I was the son of working class parents, raised in a town in which there was no shame in being a blue-collar worker or a secretary or a clerical worker. My dad was a factory laborer, an uncle a clerical worker, an aunt a secretary, another uncle a construction laborer, many cousins coal miners, factory hands, and truck drivers. At the college, I was shocked and angered to see displays of superiority by anyone toward a co-worker. I was friendly to the people who cleaned my office, typed my exams, and cut the grass outside our buildings. Working people often feel socially inferior to "professional" workers. My mother always exclaims in wonder when I tell her about some of the disgusting and foolish things I have seen teachers do. "But they're educated," she says, "They have PhDs." Yet she remains inordinately proud that I am a college professor and is automatically respectful to my colleagues. She feels especially good if a professional worker is nice to her, and I have found this to be the case for most working people. So my friendliness toward other workers on campus was returned.

I was always in my office, working on the interminable lectures at all hours. The custodians in my building stopped in at least once a day to empty the wastebaskets. As we exchanged pleasantries and they found out what I taught, they began to complain about their jobs. One of them, Mike, had been a union coal miner and was critical of the low wages, constantly changing shifts, and favoritism shown by the foreman. The other custodian, Jane, was less forthcoming at first; she was afraid that any comments she made would get back to the boss. Gradually, she opened up and voiced most of Mike's grievances and some others, including the fact that women were being discriminated against in terms of pay and job offerings. Within a few months, Mike was saying that they needed a union. Jane agreed. They asked if I could help, and I said I would.

To our surprise, we could not get a local union to help organize the forty-three workers who cleaned and maintained the buildings and grounds. Too many unions look at a small workplace, or bargaining unit, as it is called under the law, and make the business decision that it is not "cost effective" to organize such a group. After much effort, we finally got the union that had already organized similar workers at the central campus of the university to lead our organizing drive. We called a meeting at a local motel, and nearly three-quarters of the workers came and participated in a frank discussion of their work. After this we distributed authorization cards, cards saying that the worker authorized the union to represent him or her. We needed at least thirty percent of the employees to sign these before we could petition the Labour Board for an election. Within two weeks, more than fifty percent had signed, and we asked for an election.

The college's administrators knew of our campaign soon after it began. In every shop there are company stool pigeons. Two brothers who were custodians were promised better jobs by the foreman if they would oppose the union. Ironically, after the union won the election, the foreman forgot about his promises, and the men promptly became staunch union supporters, one of them serving as shop steward for many years.

Once the administration learned about the union drive, it went on the offensive to defeat it. The university's commitment to freedom of expression proved not to extend to its employees. The foreman spied on the janitors at night and early in the morning to make sure they punched in on time and were hard at work. Special focus was put on the women, because the employer thought they were the most vulnerable. The foreman told the women who cleaned the dormitories that they would lose certain privileges if a union got in, such as the freedom to check into work late when they had to get their kids ready for school.

The anti-union attacks escalated. Workers received letters from administrators, warning them about the dire consequences of a union. They were told that a union was an outsider that would interfere with the personal relationships between the employees and their supervisors. Workers could always come to their foreman and talk about problems, and the college would do everything in its power to correct them. Such letters were addressed, "Dear Fellow Employee." These missives were sent by an administrator who had merely signed a letter written by the university's attorneys. Later, when the teachers organized, the chancellor of the university sent us letters with the salutation, "Dear Colleague." He had an enormous salary, a free house, and a staff of servants. His underlings even ordered his restaurant meals in advance so that he would not have to wait to eat. Subsequently, when it was discovered that he had profited personally at university expense, the Board of Trustees did not summarily fire him as they would have any of his "dear colleagues." His departure was cushioned by the golden parachute they had secretly agreed to give him upon his retirement.

Right before the election, a supervisor called a mandatory meeting during the mid-afternoon shift change where he assailed the union and attacked me specifically. He said I was a communist and that the workers ought to be careful with me. He claimed that I had my own agenda and did not have their interests at heart. As the election got closer, threats that the workers would lose benefits and favors became more strident. It never seemed to occur to the administrators that the men and women who kept the physical plant running and had keys to all the offices were intelligent enough to make their own decision about how they wanted to deal with the administration. In everything they did during the union campaign, the employer acted as if it believed that these workers were more like children than adults—unruly, under the sway of their passions, and in need of guidance. The dean told me that I could not use the school's copying machine to make copies of pro-union propaganda. I asked him why administrators could use them but not those who supported the workers. He had no answer, so I ignored his command.

The election was held in the summer, and we made sure that those on vacation or sick leave got to the polling station on campus. The university poll watchers were confident of victory; they had not lost to a union in a long time. Everyone voted, and the board agent counted the ballots on the spot. We were as nervous as cats as the votes were placed into two piles—yeses and nos. As we watched the size of each pile, it became apparent that we not only had won, but by a large margin. Now the workers had a weapon to change their working lives. Time would tell how well they used it. But for the moment, these forty-three poorly paid and hard-working members of the working class had defeated their social betters, the high-priced administrators and lawyers who thought of the janitors and groundskeeper as a faceless and docile mass, unworthy of their respect.

Soon after this election, some of us began to say that the teachers needed a union too. The situation seemed ripe. Several young and better-educated faculty members had been hired, threatening the older teachers. Both groups proved fertile grounds for organizing—the newly hired teachers because the place was so underfunded and paternalistically run, and the senior faculty because they felt menaced by the sharp changes taking place. I became friendly with the new teachers, especially an anthropology instructor who had shocked the dean at a faculty meeting during his first year by suggesting that the wishes of the students should be considered before we took some action. I remember heads turning to see who this unusual person was, since no one ever said anything controversial at a faculty meeting. We began to go out for drinks after our night class, and soon we were plotting to unionize the faculty. We contacted one of the teachers' unions and arranged to have an informational meeting on campus. We sent out fliers to each teacher. I was president of the local chapter of the American Association of University Professors (AAUP), an organization aimed at protecting faculty rights, and I used this to justify holding the meeting. Our AAUP group had just completed a salary survey whose results shocked us. We found that salaries were amazingly low and horribly disparate.

Women were paid much less than men, and it was apparent that all sorts of special deals had been cut. One woman with twenty-six years of teaching experience was making less than most newly hired teachers. Married faculty made more than the unmarried, presumably on the assumption that a married man had a family to support. We used the survey results to justify the union meeting. We would learn about unions and see whether one could rectify the gross injustices shown in the salary survey.

We were to meet the union organizers at a local motel, but they were late and we had to get back to the meeting room, which was in one of the classroom buildings. The room was packed, a remarkable thing, since it was May and the regular school year was over. I went to the front of the room and explained that the speakers would be late. Startlingly, a teacher sitting in the back, one of the most senior faculty members in the school and the former mayor of the town, started to heckle me. He made ugly remarks about me and about unions. It hit me that he had been sent by the administration to disrupt the meeting, and he was doing a good job of it. He managed to put me in a state of panic. I kept order as best I could, and luckily the speakers arrived and took control. We had a sharp discussion and, after the meeting, decided to send out authorization cards and call another meeting.

The cards began to dribble in, with nothing like the speed in which the janitors and groundskeeper had sent in theirs. The professor who had tried to disrupt the meeting began talking to the faculty; he had many supporters, mostly older teachers, many of whom had made private deals with the administration. I began to learn the art of compromise. I wanted a union, but I had no respect for the old guard. With a few notable exceptions they were incompetent in the extreme and socially reactionary. Yet, to keep the cards coming in, I had to show a certain amount of deference to them, even the scoundrel who tried to provoke a melee at the meeting. By the start of the fall term, we had enough cards to petition the Labour Board for an election.

The university fought our union efforts. After our first meeting, I was called in to see the college president. He was new to the school, a military man and friend of the university's chancellor, brought in to oversee the transformation of the college from a two-year junior college to a four-year school. His secretary phoned on a Friday afternoon and wanted me to come to his office immediately. I told her that I was busy and couldn't see the president until Monday. I knew the purpose of the meeting and did not want to give him an edge.

When we met on Monday, the first thing the president said was, "What do the teachers want?" I said that the fact that he did not know was good proof that things were in a bad way. We chatted amiably for a few minutes, and I left. The next year, we organized a vote of no confidence in him that I read at the faculty meeting. Not long after that, he went back to a less visible but more powerful job at the central university. He never said much about the union drive; the administrative strategy to defeat us was quickly channeled into the legal arena.

The United States has a wide array of labour laws, originally aimed at protecting the rights of workers to form unions, bargain with employers, labour in safe work places, be protected from overwork, and be paid at least a minimum wage. When workers have been strongly organized, these laws have been adequately enforced. But organized labour began a long period of decline after the Second World War, and the laws were amended to help employers, interpreted in a pro-employer way by the courts, and inadequately enforced. Today, the law provides numerous ways for an employer to defeat a union. Many of these involve techniques of delay. Employers know that if they can delay a union certification election or collective bargaining, they have a good chance to defeat the union. As they say, "Justice delayed is justice denied."

Under U.S. labour law, the bargaining unit (the group of employees who bargains with the employer) must be "appropriate," that is, one which will allow for adequate representation of the workers and one in which the workers have a "community of interest," that is, a cohesiveness that will allow them to bargain effectively. There is no one appropriate bargaining unit, and community of interest is usually based on similarity of working conditions and worker interaction. A standard employer tactic to fight a union is to challenge the composition or scope of the bargaining unit. The university challenged ours, which consisted of all teachers and librarians at our campus in Johnstown. The university argued that, because our campus was integrated with other parts of the university, a separate unit at Johnstown was not appropriate. In other words, it challenged the scope of the unit. It could also have argued that other groups of workers at our campus should have been included. An employer making these claims is almost in a no-lose situation. If it wins, so many additional employees will be added to the unit that the union will not have met the thirty-percent threshold, or, if it does, it no longer has majority support. If the employer loses and the unit stays the same, it has bought time to campaign against the union and allow employee enthusiasm to die down. The Labour Board called a hearing in Pittsburgh, at which the union and the employer would present evidence and make arguments about the unit.

At the hearing, the union attorney had to rely on two instructors, me and my anthropologist friend, to refute the university's arguments. The university was represented at the hearing by the school's most senior administrators and a battery of lawyers from Pittsburgh's largest law firm, one which had originally served people like Andrew Carnegie and Henry Clay Frick, architects of the bloody defeat of the steelworkers' union at Homestead in 1892. My friend and I tried to locate documentation to show that our campus administration made enough independent decisions and our faculty was separate enough from those in other parts of the university to give us sufficient community of interest to justify a separate bargaining unit. We were in no position to uncover official university documents to this effect, so we put together whatever we could find. Unfortunately, the state law that governed our union rights (we were public employees and not covered by the national law) also protected the employer against a proliferation of bargaining units. If we were allowed to have a separate unit at Johnstown, the university might then have had to face many other independent bargaining units, since there are numerous schools and colleges within the university.

The hearing was a fiasco for us. At its start, I heard an administrator, a man who had been recently fired as president of another college, exclaim, "Him again," when he saw me. He remembered me from the hearing for the maintenance and custodial workers. Later, in the hallway during a break, we overheard him say, "Who do those punks think they are?" He seemed astounded that two lowly untenured instructors had the audacity to challenge the mighty university. My poor buddy found out just how tough his bosses were. We chose him to present our testimony, while I sat at the attorney's side feeding him questions and information. The university's attorney subjected Bruce to a withering cross-examination, reducing him to the small cog in the gigantic corporate machinery he was. "Exactly how was he in a position to know that what he had testified to was true," the lawyer asked. "Was he an officer of the university, or even a top administrator?" Bruce answered "no," making it impossible for us to win the case. We called some university officials to testify as hostile witnesses, but they hewed the company line. We could not prove that they were being less than honest, because we were not in an official position to know. It was a catch-22. We were in over our heads, legally speaking.

A few weeks after the hearing, the Labour Board ruled against us, dooming our union drive. The only appropriate bargaining unit was one which was university-wide. A union movement developed among the entire university faculty a few years later. The university again challenged the proposed bargaining unit, and it took twenty-six hearing days and a million taxpayer dollars to resolve this issue. Despite this delay, we eventually got an election, but the movement had fractured into competing union groupings. Three unions vied for faculty allegiance, and each spent as much time bashing its rivals as it did the administration. The three unions combined polled 51 percent of the vote on the first ballot, but more teachers voted "no union" than voted for any one of the unions. There was then a runoff between the union that got the most votes and "no union," and the union was defeated handily. Sadly, Bruce and I supported different unions and nearly got into a fist fight in the dining room arguing over which union was better. It took us awhile to patch up our friendship.

The difference between the two campaigns taught me something about the consciousness of workers. The maintenance and custodial employees saw themselves as labourers, more or less stuck in circumstances that they could not individually improve. Many teachers did not think of themselves like this, and if they did, would have been too embarrassed to say so. I felt like a worker, more privileged than the other campus workers but just as much subject to arbitrary employer authority. However, many teachers would have denied this, instead believing themselves to be independent professionals. To admit that they needed a union would have been to shatter their self-image.

Bowling Alley

NON-FICTION

It was a mid-Sunday afternoon in late winter. We had just finished our match, and I was disappointed with my poor performance. For some reason, I could not prevent my left wrist from turning over when I released my bowling ball, and this caused it to hook disastrously to the right. My teammates groaned as my scores plummeted about forty pins below my average and our chances of winning the league championship melted away. It wasn't a cutthroat league, so they commiserated as I packed away my equipment and put on my coat to leave. As I passed by the manager's desk, I glanced up at the television set on the wall. A professional basketball game was in progress, and, since I am a basketball junky, I stopped to watch. The Chicago Bulls were playing the Boston Celtics. I disliked the Celtics and their rabid fans and arrogant general manager and former coach, Red Auerbach. I was gratified to see that the Bulls' star, Michael Jordan, was playing a spectacular game, on his way to scoring more than sixty points in what turned out to be a double-overtime, Celtics victory.

Another man was watching the game, along with his young son. I recognized him—an average bowler and delivery truck driver, something of a loudmouth with a higher opinion of his bowling skills than his ability warranted. Normally I would have ignored him, but Jordan's great game was so exciting that I just had to say something about it. So I said, "Boy, isn't he an amazing player."

This innocent remark sent the man into a tirade. "That nigger's not the best player. The best player is that white guy, Larry Bird." Now, Johnstown is a racist town. It is almost impossible to go into a bar in a white neighborhood and not hear the word "nigger" within thirty minutes. While warming up before a basketball pickup game, one of my students commented that he liked the Boston Celtics because they were the "white team." In 1922, the mayor of Johnstown ordered all black residents who had not lived in the town for at least five years to leave. Black men had been recruited to work in the city by the steel companies in the wake of the bitter 1919 strike, and the mayor issued his order after an incident involving a black person and the police. It is not known exactly how many African Americans left town, but the growth of the black population stopped. In the 1980s, blacks comprised less than 3 percent of the city's residents.

Yet even though I had often experienced open racism in Johnstown, I was startled by this man's vehemence. His face turned red, and the veins on his neck were showing. I said, "What difference does skin color make? Jordan is a great player."

He glared at me and yelled, "Don't tell me about the niggers. I lived near them. I know what they're like. They're no fucking good."

I looked down at his son and said, "Hey, you're really setting a fine example for your kid. He'll grow up to be a bigot just like you."

At this, he lost his composure and said, "Listen, four eyes, I'll knock your fucking glasses off. I don't give a fuck who you are."

I noticed that no one at the desk was making any effort to defuse this situation. So I just said, "Go ahead and hit me if you want to." He didn't, and I picked up my bag and left.

Filmmaker Michael Moore once chided liberals for not spending much time with working people. He suggested that they go to car racetracks and bowling alleys. Moore was probably thinking of workers as the salt of the earth, the men and women who do the work. He is right, but he should remember that being a worker doesn't mean that a person's mind is clear and free of dangerous hatreds. My antagonist's racism was disgustingly blatant, but no more so than that of millions of others.

Most racism is more subtle, so woven into the fabric of everyday life that whites just take it for granted. It crosses all classes, but that of white workers is the saddest and says the most about how this economic system deforms our personalities. The man who confronted me in the bowling alley was a delivery truck driver, doing menial labour at low wages. He obviously had been poor as a child. Yet he hated the poorest and most exploited of workers. He had been led to believe that black people are the lowest of the low, and since he grew up with them, he must be contemptible himself. This filled him with shame, but he dealt with this by coming to think that black persons must in some sense be responsible for not only their own misery, but also his. His hatred transformed shame into superiority, a feeling encouraged by other whites, not least of whom were employers who used racism to drive a wedge between those whose alliance would be most dangerous to their power.

It is hard for me to think of the incident in the bowling alley without remembering all the other examples set for me by teachers, friends, clergy, and other adults. The minstrel show, my college biology teacher, the geography of my hometown. I won't deny that progress in race relations has been made, but the white suburban kids who filled my classes are still writing racist graffiti on the bathroom walls and still fuming about welfare as a code for racism in their essays. Just how different is their upbringing from mine? White people are raised to be racists, and it takes a mighty effort to overcome this. I know. I'm still trying.

Cesar

CREATIVE NON-FICTION

Author's note: I worked for the United Farm Workers Union during a sabbatical leave in the winter of 1977. I was made Research Director and spent my time investigating the growers, helping out in negotiations, and testifying in unfair labour practice cases. While I was there I witnessed disturbing events, brought on in my view by the union president's paranoia in the face of daunting external pressures. The meeting described in the story, in which several staff persons were purged from the union, was held while I was on union assignment. I learned the details of it from persons present. I re-created the meeting from information I received from them. I put myself there and invented the dialogue for dramatic effect, although some of the dialogue was told to me by friends who were there. For verification that the union behaved then and later in an unusual and, from a workers' point of view, autocratic and detrimental manner, see the series of articles in the *Los Angeles Times*, beginning at <www.latimes.com/news/local/la-me-ufw8jan08,1,7202033.story>. An earlier series was published in *The Village Voice*, in the issues of August 14 and 21, 1984. Supporting materials can also be found at <www.farmworkermovement.org>. Except for Cesar Chavez and Jane Fonda, the names in the story are not the real names of the persons described.

I drove into union headquarters at 1:15 in the morning. It was raining, and I barely saw the sign for Keene, California, which was where my directions said to turn right from Route 66. Two hours before, I had eaten at a truck stop in Needles and begun driving across the desert. Now I was in the mountains, west of Tehachapi, heading toward Bakersfield. Keene wasn't on the California map in my road atlas, so I wasn't expecting much of a town. In fact, there was no town at all, just the Keene Café, Ed and Edna Melton, proprietors. It was closed, so I couldn't stop to ask directions. I kept driving up the narrow road and, about a mile later, saw a hand-painted sign on a small post which read "La Paz: United Farm Workers of America." I turned my head back to the road just in time to brake before I ran over the guard who was flagging me to stop. He motioned me into a driveway blocked by a gate. A second guard approached my car from a small guardhouse, shined a light in my face, and asked me in a strongly accented voice what my business was. It didn't sound like they were expecting me. I found out later that the scheduled guards had been told, but they had traded shifts with two compañeros and forgotten to tell them. Ordinarily, this wouldn't have mattered, but death threats had been made against union president Chavez and the guards were cautious of strangers. I told the second guard my name, that I had come to work for the union, and that I was expected. I gave him the name of my contact, Bill Martin, the union's personnel director. He had a conversation in Spanish with the other guard, who went into the booth and made a telephone call. Then he came out and, in a friendly tone said, "Welcome to the Farm Workers."

Within minutes, Bill appeared on foot, introduced himself, said something to the guards and got into my car. "I'll show you your room. You must be tired. You can get some sleep and we'll talk tomorrow. I'll stop by for you at 7:00." I looked at my watch—2:00. I would still be tired in the morning. I had left Johnstown, Pennsylvania, on New Year's Day, 1977, with an abscessed tooth, and by the time I reached Amarillo, Texas, I was taking fifteen Aspirins a day without much effect. Suddenly, a pain shot through my jaw so sharp that I had to stifle a cry. I had a feeling that my next good night's sleep would be awhile in coming.

As he opened the door, Bill was saying something about how they hadn't had time to clean my room. I was thinking, well, how bad could it be, until I looked inside. I'm glad he didn't look at me just then because my face must have reflected my impulse to turn around and run. The room was filthy, an inch of dust on the floor, trash covering nearly every surface, furnished only with an ancient iron bed, a dirty sagging chair, and a scarred cupboard tilting dangerously forward. I wondered if maybe this was a test given to new recruits to measure their commitment. But Bill was talking cheerfully about how this was one of the nicer rooms, just a bit messy. I could get it shipshape in no time. I tried to duplicate Bill's cheerfulness. "It looks fine. Anyway, I'm so tired, I could sleep anywhere tonight. See you at seven." I lied about sleeping. No way was I going to rest now. I spent the next two hours cleaning the room as best I could, manically sweeping, shaking, and wiping. By 4:00 a.m. the room was presentable, at least in the dim light cast by the bare bulb hanging from the ceiling. I walked down the hall to the shower, but it didn't work. I washed myself with cold water, went back to my room and fell asleep. I dreamt that I was the preacher in *The Grapes of Wrath* addressing a large crowd of farm workers. I was talking about the loaves and fishes. Here in these rich valleys there were loaves and fishes aplenty, yet we who grew them went hungry. The rich men's tables were filled to overflowing, yet ours were bare. Where was the justice in that? The growers were like vampires sucking our blood, and it couldn't be the will of Jesus, that poor savior of us all, that we just sit here and take it. The faces in the crowd nodded approval. I could feel their power. One of them shouted out, "Hey preacher, don't forget, we want clean rooms too."

"You probably won't be able to start working right away. Each new staff person has to meet with Cesar first, and he won't be back until next week." This was disappointing news. Bill had indeed knocked on my door at seven. He had taken me to his "kitchen" for coffee, introduced me to some of his friends, and escorted me on a tour of the grounds. The union's headquarters were located in what had been a private sanitarium for alcoholics. The owner, the son of an actor of some notoriety, had donated it to the union, making him about as popular as anthrax among the local cattle and horse ranchers. It was an isolated place, tucked into the desert mountains along the railroad tracks, about two miles from the famous horseshoe curve. The sanitarium had consisted of a large hospital and several outbuildings. Single staff persons lived in the hospital, while married staff lived in small houses or trailers.

Living arrangements were varied and informal. At one time, evening meals had been taken communally in a large refectory, but chronic labour shortages had made it impossible to continue this practice. Now staff persons were responsible for their own provisioning and cooking. In the hospital, people had formed "kitchens" of six to twelve members who constituted a sort of mini-collective for shopping and cooking. Bill invited me to join his kitchen, an offer I quickly accepted. He explained that my duties would include preparing supper for eight to ten people two or three times a month and collecting money and shopping for food maybe once a month. Over coffee, I surveyed the kitchen. There was a double hotplate, an electric frying pan, a coffee pot, a few pots, pans, and plates, a motley and small collection of utensils, a beat up table, six broken chairs, a small bathroom sink, and an ancient refrigerator. No stove, no real sink, and, as I was casually informed, no hot water, which didn't matter because the water was contaminated and had to be boiled anyway. My stomach churned in panic. I couldn't cook for eight people in Julia Child's kitchen, let alone here. When a woman sitting with us pointed to the cooking sign-up sheet on the refrigerator and suggested that I might as well sign it now, I looked at her with glazed eyes. There was a hint of sarcasm in her voice. She knew I was in trouble and was enjoying it. She had frowned when Bill had invited me to join their group. Mechanically, I surveyed the sheet and, with relief, I saw that there were open days at the end of the month. I marked them and made a mental note to write to my mother for recipes.

I wondered aloud what I was supposed to do until I could meet with Cesar. Bill suggested that I introduce myself to as many people as possible and let them know that I was available for work. He had heard that I would be working in the research office. Cesar had seemed excited when Bill had shown him my application. Bill had read it and decided that my skills might be better used here at union headquarters than in the Detroit boycott office, which was where I had originally been assigned. Cesar agreed, and this pleased Bill greatly. Cesar had said that we can get professors on our side, too.

Most of the people I met that first week were new, and there were frequent references to people who had just left. This didn't surprise me — low wages, hard work, and crummy living conditions have a way of wearing down people's commitment. The new people were uniformly idealistic and happy to be here. Most were in their early twenties and had supported the union in college or in their churches. To all of us the union was special, an uncorrupted champion of the poorest workers, and Cesar was a hero, a mystical little man, a modern-day Gandhi who, through sheer determination and will, had finally beaten the growers. He had built a union and a movement. The campesinos flocked to his union, and people who wanted to do something right with their lives flocked to his movement. With monastic zeal we came to the union, to do good and, I suppose, to purify our souls.

On first meeting, union veterans seemed just as idealistic and selfless as the newcomers. Within a few days I felt more at home than I imagined possible. This was a true community, and I found myself thinking that I should quit teaching and live here. I felt separated from my former self, as if I were in the middle of a spiritual reawakening. One evening, a married couple took me to a local union meeting in a small town down the mountain. About two hundred workers talked and sang in Spanish and English, loyalists, none of whom had yet won union contracts but who had marched and picketed from San Francisco to Boston, giving witness for the union. "Yo soy economista," I repeated again and again. They smiled a silent welcome or told me their stories in broken English. I was moved, happy to be with brothers and sisters.

"You can go in now." I had been waiting in Cesar's outer office for an hour, ignored by his personal secretary, a young Anglo named Mark Wilson. Mark was flanked by two assistants, another Anglo and a handsome Chicano, Juan Salazar, who was Cesar's chief bodyguard. They were not a friendly group. They made me uncomfortable, especially Mark, who struck me as a person who feels he has the right to order people around because he is close to the person who can. When Juan looked at me, I remembered that I had seen him the night before arguing with a woman I assumed to be his wife. Their child was crying and his wife was saying loudly that he should spend more time with his son. Juan spoke sharply to her—when he saw me, he glared but then smiled and said, "Buenos noches, hermano." Today, I remembered the glare.

My meeting lasted less than five minutes. Mark followed me into a spare, windowless office and introduced me to Cesar. He was a small, slightly built man with jet black hair, dressed in a cheap open-collared shirt, chino pants, and sandals. He shook my hand limply but with both hands. He had a gentle voice and manner. He spoke directly and without pause, explaining what he had in mind for me to do. He wanted me to attend a staff conference the following weekend. Then the meeting was over. At the door I turned to ask a question. Cesar looked up at me from his desk. I was too embarrassed to speak so I smiled and left.

Stockton is about forty miles east of San Francisco, a shabby town, squat and dirty, like most of those in California's central valleys. In summer the temperature reaches 110 degrees, and the air is fouled by pesticides. We had arrived in Stockton late at night after a long drive: Cesar, two bodyguards, and me. We stayed at the house of a union supporter. Cesar knew thousands of people and, like an Indian holy man, never had to worry about a place to eat and sleep. It was my thirty-first birthday, and I had packed a bottle of wine. We drank it after the meal and a meeting with a union lawyer. Cesar toasted me. He said that I was doing good work for the union.

My job in Stockton was to testify in an unfair labour practice hearing. Under pressure from the union, its allies, and a sympathetic governor, California's legislature had enacted a law that gave farm workers the right to organize unions and negotiate contracts without employer interference. Most growers had reacted to the law with contempt and continued to treat their workers like peons and unions as the work of communist agitators. Once the union had organized a ranch, it had to get the employer to the bargaining table. More often than not, the growers refused to go.

Stockton was a hotbed of grower defiance of the law, complete with terrorist vigilante groups. The alleged leader of the vigilantes was one Ernest Carvalho Jr., a tomato grower and labour contractor. Mr. Carvalho had a fearsome reputation, having once yanked a union organizer up from the ground by his mustache. He had met the server of a labour board subpoena with a shotgun. During the organizing campaign, two of his workers, union supporters, had been savagely beaten. No one doubted that the attacker had been paid by Carvalho. Miraculously, the union had won the election, but Carvalho had refused to recognize and bargain with it, forcing the union to file charges. My job was to testify as to how much money Carvalho's refusal to bargain had cost the campesinos. Cesar would testify, too, because this was the first case of its kind. A large judgment against the grower would send a strong message to others.

We arrived at the municipal building early. Our lawyers had to talk to some of the witnesses, farm workers huddled in a group at the rear of the room. They were tense and fearful, but the sight of Cesar eased them greatly. He had a bond with them difficult to describe but readily seen. He was of them but above them. He was their leader; he had asked them to be here; they were here. As he spoke with them, I thought of the Zapatistas in Orozco's painting. Like them, these campesinos stood straight and tall in front of their commander, in sharp contrast to their stooped and suppliant bodies out in the fields.

By the start of the hearing, the small room was packed. The rows of folding chairs were separated by a narrow centre aisle. We sat on the left, Carvalho and company on the right. I read a book once that said that *The Grapes of Wrath* was not a great novel, because the growers were presented as one-dimensionally evil people. The writer should have seen this crew. Big-bellied, fat-jowled, cold-eyed men dressed in jeans and boots and cowboy hats, sniggering among themselves, giving us hard stares. They looked exactly like pigs, and Carvalho was their pig-leader. When I glanced at him, I had an image of him strangling Cesar with his bare hands, grunting, spit dripping from his chin. I was sure that he stank no matter how many showers he took. No, these were evil people. They were capable of unprovoked violence. Had I thought about it, I would have argued that Steinbeck had been too generous. Because up and down the valleys there are men like these. They are the bedrock of California agriculture, the shock troops for the big corporate growers with their smooth-as-silk lawyers and suave manners, who wouldn't think of beating or hitting a farm worker but wouldn't mourn her death either.

The hearing was raucous and unruly. We petitioned to have testimony translated into Spanish, but the judge refused. He said we would never finish a bilingual hearing, but then he had to admonish us to keep quiet a dozen times as we whispered translations to the campesinos. Carvalho stood up and shouted that he "wasn't gonna negotiate with no bunch of god-dam comanists." He said, "I'm just a dumb fuckin' Portagee, but I ain't dealin' with no comanists." When the judge warned him about his language, he grinned and said, "I don't know no other words. I'm just a dumb Portagee." His lawyer tried to calm him, but Carvalho shoved him away. He pointed at Cesar and taunted, "Hey Cesar. Let's me and you settle this. Let's go in the next room. Me and you. If you come out first, I'll recognize your commie union. If I come out, hey, we'll just all go home and forget this fuckin' hearing." Cesar sat immobile and stared ahead, but his bodyguards tensed. The judge kept pounding his gavel, but his power had deserted him. I turned to watch the other growers. The only thin man among them returned my stare with a grin. He made his hand into a gun and silently pulled the trigger. Carvalho said, "See, you're not a man, just a fuckin' comanist." The judge recessed the hearing until the next morning. When the union asked for Carvalho's employment records, which had been subpoenaed and which he had brought with him in a large cardboard box, Carvalho snapped them up and strode out of the room.

Cesar was not a good speaker. His voice was soft, and he possessed none of the tricks of the speaker's trade: the pregnant pause, the change of rhythm, the crescendo, the pointing finger. He was utterly without physical powers. Yet right away, he captivated you, made you listen, made you want to do what he said. He had a way of making you feel like an important person, that what you were telling him could change the course of the union, put it over the top of that long hill it had been climbing so slowly. Maybe it was his eyes. They were guileless eyes, the eyes of a child. You could not refuse them.

He was a master of symbolic action. He often played the saint, fasting like Gandhi, adding power by subtracting it. He would carry a cross on Good Friday, staggering under its weight, suffering for those whose lives are bounded by the short-handled hoe, the endless march, the early death. Once he had to appear in court to answer charges that union members had ambushed a train and shot rifle bullets into refrigerator cars. The local papers were full of righteous editorials and grower letters accusing the union of shameful hypocrisy, preaching but not practising non-violence. On the day of the hearing, some two thousand members and supporters lined the street leading up to the county courthouse and the steps and hallways leading to the courtroom. Cesar walked between them, staggering from a recent fast. The crowd remained eerily silent; only Cesar and the police moved. When he reached the topmost step, everyone knelt down, in unison, with machine-like precision. Within an hour, all the charges were dropped.

Every Saturday afternoon, we went out to the fields surrounding our compound to work in the garden. Sometimes this would be preceded by a community meeting. Presumably, these were town meetings in which we would air our grievances and collectively govern ourselves. But while we would act like brothers and sisters, we were the children of Cesar. He ran the meetings, and we discussed what he wanted to discuss. Flanked by his farting and belching guard dogs, Cesar would command us, cajole us, mock us, threaten us, all the while pretending that everyone was equal. I loved these meetings at first, but I soon noticed that it was dangerous to criticize Cesar. Once he told us that a friend of the union wanted to donate several washing machines and dryers, but he wasn't sure he would accept them because we wouldn't take care of them. We'd fucked up everything else. We couldn't keep the place clean. There was dog shit all over the place. Around the room hands shot up. Did Cesar realize that we had to drive fifteen miles to do laundry, which meant we had to have access to a car. And laundry cost money, which nobody had. One person's complaint gave the next person courage, and soon the room was a babble of complaining voices. Cesar was unimpressed. He said that he really didn't care about this chickenshit. He didn't have to worry about his laundry anyway. This macho response was met by a chorus of boos. Cesar's eyes narrowed and his mouth tightened. He spat out, "I work eighteen fucking hours a day, every day. For the union. Which of you can say the same? You're wasting my time with this chickenshit." We sat very still for more than a minute. Ricardo Reyes, the union's treasurer, said, "Cesar, don't forget about the water." Cesar's voice softened and he told us that we could once again drink the water. With that the meeting ended.

I liked the gardening, at least in small doses. It was good to use my muscles after sitting at a desk all week. And working on a community project with a melting pot of humanity—Filipinos, Mexicans, Anglos, men and women, young and old—gave me a feeling that the muck and slime of the real world could be overcome and, as the song went, "peace will rule the planet and love will steer the stars." Cesar loved the garden. He was an expert on organic gardening and lectured us about its subtleties, from the proper fertilizer to planting by the moon. After a while we would break for a picnic lunch, and he would tell us something of the history of the union. We were eager disciples. He spun his stories of the growers and the campesinos as Christ must have told his parables. People lowered their heads to hide their tears.

Then we had to return to work, monotonous and physically exhausting in the 80-degree February heat and high altitude. Guilt kept me hard at it, long after the warm glow of brotherhood had worn off. I wanted nothing more than to go back to my room, shower, change clothes, and begin my "day off." I would race down the mountain to Bakersfield, which, after a week of isolation at La Paz, had been transformed in my mind from the nation's biggest truck stop, carrot capital of the world, and birthplace of Merle Haggard, into a shining metropolis. I would rent a room in the Downtowner Motel, order cartons of Chinese food, eat myself sick, take a long bath, and sleep until noon. Or I'd take some friends and go to a Mexican bar to shoot pool and drink beer. We could go to a place where we would be the only Anglos and not worry about a racial confrontation because we were with the union, though it wasn't wise to root against the Mexican boxer who would be fighting on the television above the bar. Only a few more wheelbarrows of manure. Only a few more blisters on my hand. I was glad I had a little money and happy I wasn't a farm worker.

As best I can tell, the trouble began with the mail announcement. I had been in Oxnard helping a union local negotiate a piece rate proposal with a tomato grower. The grower, William Fontin, prided himself as an intellectual, a libertarian who loved Barry Goldwater and William F. Buckley. More than a few economists are libertarians. They babble about free markets and free choice and individual liberty, but when their privileges are threatened, as when the lower orders have the nerve to form, say, a union, they are quick to put on their jackboots and goose step. Fontin was no exception, although I was amused by the slogan he had printed on every box of his tomatoes, "Unsubsidized Product of the Free Capitalist Economy of the United States." He smoked a pipe and was usually polite, but he would agree to nothing. He refused to negotiate in Spanish though he spoke it fluently. He referred to me as "that professor of yours." I had gotten to know the union negotiating team. The handsome president of the committee had invited me to a party at his house where I'd gotten drunk enough on tequila to dance. I wanted to help, but we were just going through the motions. Fontin was as tough as Carvalho. He wouldn't settle until the workers showed that they could make his tomatoes rot on the vine.

When I returned to La Paz, I heard about the mail fiasco from two of my friends, Daniel and Carl. They came to my room, looking up and down the hall before closing the door. "Did you hear about the mail shit?" asked Daniel. "Orders from Cesar. From now on all of your mail is going to be opened before you get it."

"You're kidding," I said, wondering to myself if anything in any letters to me could be suspect. "Why?"

"They say it's because some contributions people sent to the union are missing, but that's bullshit. It's just more of Cesar's paranoia."

I had been waiting for something bad to happen. Right before I had gone off to do the piece rate proposal, Cesar had asked for volunteers to participate in a retreat at a drug and alcohol rehabilitation clinic run by a friend of his. This place, Dalanon, had achieved some notoriety complete with an exposé in the local newspapers. The founder, Ron Wood, had become something of a guru and his organization a spiritual centre with its own unique methods for curing drug addiction. Each newly admitted addict was compelled to participate in the "game," as Ron called it. The game was nothing more than a thought control device, common to many cults. People in the group would gang up on the new people, accusing them of all sorts of bad deeds while at the same time giving them maximum attention. Combined with sleep deprivation and a bad diet, this regimen often succeeded in making people feel helpless unless they gave themselves up to the group. Given a benign reading, this may be just what a person ruined by drugs needs, a new life so to speak. A more cynical person might see in this a form of mind control aimed primarily at enhancing the power of the leader. My instinct told me that the latter interpretation was more likely to be true. My gut reaction was reinforced when someone told me that Ron's disciples had placed a poisonous snake in the mailbox of the reporter who had written the exposé. Ominously, the people chosen to be in the game were all in Cesar's inner circle of relatives, bodyguards, and personal aides.

Gossip about the mail and the game abounded. A young maintenance worker, Roger, boldly posted a petition protesting the opening of our mail. I signed it, and so did most of my friends. This created tension. People began to avoid us, and most people

stopped talking about anything that had to do with the union. I
began to suspect that Cesar's bodyguards were watching us carefully. One of them mysteriously showed up at the first session of
a labour history class that some staff had asked me to teach. No
one with whom I was close volunteered for the game.

The tension was broken somewhat by two events—Cesar's
fiftieth birthday party and the trip to Los Angeles to campaign
for the mayor. Hundreds of notables came to the party. We
started it out at six o'clock in the morning with a serenade at
Cesar's house, complete with mariachi band and shots of tequila. Then we ate menudo (tripe soup) to ward off the effects
of the liquor and took up our posts at the giant barbecue in
honor of our leader. My job was to dole out the sauce, a fiery
concoction that went on the meat and rice. The Anglos would
say "not too much," but the Mexicans would say "más, más."
During a break, I went to my office to get a book, and I came
upon Jane Fonda, the famous actress and brave critic of the war
in Vietnam, bitching at her kids for tormenting Cesar's dogs.
"Can't you children behave anywhere?" she moaned. Even the
rich and famous have their troubles, I thought. I stumbled
into bed hours later and fell right to sleep. But I was awakened
too soon by the sounds of loud talking from the room across
the hall. I put my ear up to my door and listened. I recognized
the voices of two of Cesar's bodyguards. They were giving the
third degree to Chris, one of the union's youngest volunteers.
"Why did you sign the mail petition? You called Cesar a dictator! Man, you're a fucking traitor. Cesar wants you out of here.
Tomorrow." When they left, I quietly went back to bed, too
afraid to go over and comfort Chris.

The next week Cesar pulled the entire staff out of headquarters and into an abandoned high school in East Los Angeles.
From there we were sent into the streets with farm workers
from throughout the state to march door-to-door, urging people to vote for the incumbent mayor. As usual, Cesar gave us
no warning, just orders. Some of the older staff were upset by

this. The union had more pressing business, namely scores of organizing drives and numerous contracts to negotiate. They wondered aloud why we were doing this instead, especially since the mayor had little competition and eventually won by a large margin. I, too, thought that the trip was unnecessary, but the whole thing again demonstrated Cesar's amazing ability to get people to do what he wanted and the union's capacity to organize complex logistics on short notice. East Los Angeles was fascinating, like being in another country. The tiny houses and shabby apartments and hotels exuded poverty, but the pastel colors and warm breezes deceived you. Somehow tropical poverty didn't seem as real from the outside as did the slums of the great Eastern cities. As I chatted in my bad Spanish with the campesina with whom I had been paired, I wondered what would happen when we got back to La Paz.

Cesar marched into the community meeting room followed by four of his bodyguards. Usually he chatted with someone seated in front and waited for us to stop talking so that the meeting could begin. But this time he just stood and stared at us, as did the guards. From the rear came voices urging quiet. I looked around the room. It was jammed; people were standing in the doorway on tiptoes craning to see. The sudden quiet was eerie because it was so unusual. Even the babies and young children were silent. The last sound I heard was a guitar chord. We always sang songs at our meetings, "No Nos Moverán" or "De Colores," but there would be no singing tonight.

"Some people here are trying to undermine the union." Cesar said this without emotion but he might as well have screamed at us. I felt a knot forming in my stomach, and my throat became dry. I noticed that the bodyguards were still standing; two were wearing dark glasses, reminding me of Tonton Macoutes. Something was terribly wrong. "There's a cancer growing in the union. We know now that some people have gone over to the growers. We go to a fucking meeting and they knew our proposals. We plan to organize a ranch and they know about it before we fucking start. Some people here are traitors. And they're going to have to leave."

"Who are these bastards, Cesar?" asked the chubby old man sitting next to me. He was a Filipino, Ricardo Ochoco, an officer of the union who had defended Cesar's tirade about the washing machines. There was a certain tension between Filipinos and Hispanics rooted in the fact that while the Filipino minority had actually started the union, the Hispanic majority, led by Cesar, had taken control of it, some said in a less than democratic manner. Cesar always spoke highly of the Filipino brothers and sisters, and Ochoco was proof of the multi-ethnic leadership of the union. But Ochoco was a weak man, a sycophant always trying to prove his loyalty to Cesar.

"Wait a minute, Cesar, how do you know..." Juan Reyes, a tough little Chicano and chief of the maintenance staff, jumped up to ask a question, but he was drowned out before he could finish by shouts that seemed to come from all around the room.

"Juan is one of them."

"He's always complaining. His name is first on the mail protest."

"He called Cesar a dictator."

To my right, Nico, Cesar's youngest son, stood up and yelled, "Listen, listen." He reminded me of a puppet, waving his hands. Nico had never impressed me. He was a whiny teenager with an unpleasant nasal voice and without much talent. Like most of Cesar's inner circle, his main virtue was doing what his father wanted. Like them, he was nothing without Cesar.

"Listen, I think Juan is selling out the union. Juan Salazar saw him in Bakersfield talking to some growers. He's one of the leaders of a clique here, always badmouthing the union. At every meeting he opposes Cesar. He's a fucking traitor."

At this, Juan Reyes made a rush for Nico but was quickly surrounded by the guards. "That's a bunch of fucking lies," he shouted. I waited for others to defend Juan, but none did. Those who weren't shouting insults at him sat rigidly on the uncomfortable seats. They were afraid, and I was too. "Let him go." Cesar commanded. He walked over to Juan Reyes and said quietly, "Brother, you're screwing the union. It would be better if you left." Juan looked at him in disbelief. He was close to tears. I waited for him to respond, but he didn't. He just walked out of the room.

Before anyone could react, Maria Quiñones was pointing a finger at David Young who was sitting next to me. "David is always with Juan Reyes. He's a traitor too." David tensed and looked at her. He had contempt for Maria, as did I. She was the daughter of the union's first vice president, Domenica Quiñones, a legendary union organizer who had faced down more than one gun and had been arrested countless times. But Maria was not the equal of her mother. She was nosy and obnoxious, La Casa's telephone operator and notorious for listening in on our calls. She often slept with Charlie, the guard, who occupied the room above me, keeping me awake with their noisy quarrels and lovemaking. Outside the union she was just another unpleasant person. You could ignore her. But here she was important. She could ruin your life, and she had just begun to ruin David's.

"You're full of shit," David said, but his words were drowned out by accusations from every corner of the room. The same stock phrases hurled at Juan Reyes were now directed at David. It struck me suddenly that this had all been planned. This was "the game." This was what they had learned at Dalanon. I was witnessing the transformation of the union into a cult. A sense of detachment came over me, and I watched the show trial unfolding before me as if I were watching a horror movie, afraid but curious to see what would happen.

David stood up and demanded, "Am I on trial here. What are the charges, Cesar?"

"Isn't it true that you said that campaigning for Mayor Bradley was a waste of time?" Cesar was agitated and speaking in an uncharacteristically loud voice.

"So what. So did lots of people."

"Haven't you been criticizing me, saying chickenshit stuff behind my back, saying it was my fault the union lost the Initiative?"

"That's bullshit. Who told you that, that fucking wimp over there." David pointed at Nico, who took his cue to launch into a tirade, accusing David of being an agent for the growers. Other voices joined the chorus. No one spoke in David's defense.

Before he could be stopped, David hopped over two rows of chairs and stood next to Cesar. No one made a move to subdue him. "Am I being charged?" David asked. He was standing straight, almost at attention, dwarfing the diminutive Cesar beside him. The guards made a move toward him, but Cesar waved them away. David's actions had surprised him, threatening to unravel this carefully choreographed meeting. It was up to the rest of us now. Many of us were David's friends. None of us believed that he was an agent of the grower or anything else but a brother dedicated to the union. But he could never stand up to Cesar alone. Would we defend him?

"The union constitution says that no one can be expelled without a fair hearing. What are the charges against me? Who is making them? I have a right to defend myself. This whole thing here tonight is illegal."

"You don't have any fucking rights, brother. You're working for the growers. We know it. You're a cancer here, a disease. Admit it, man. Hey, let's put it to a vote, right here. Who thinks David should go?"

The same voices that had been yelling for blood all night cried out in unison, "Go. Go. Go." Some others joined the chorus. Mark Wilson, Carlos's secretary, began to clap his hands. Soon the chanting and clapping filled the room, the noise rising to a fearsome level. Sweat glistened on the blank faces of the believers; they were in the grip of a religious frenzy. They wanted blood, and they would have it.

Suddenly, Cesar raised his hands and silenced the howling mob. "Who thinks David should stay?" No one raised a hand. The ferocity of the crowd cowed us completely. I thought, maybe he is guilty. I was grateful that it wasn't me. I looked at Sister Denise. She was looking at me with sad and frightened eyes. Then she raised her hand. Cesar's eyes blazed at her with hatred, but he quickly looked away.

"See, brother. The community wants you to leave. Leave now brother." Cesar then addressed us in his usual soft voice. "This meeting is over. Don't forget. We'll be going to the garden tomorrow after mass." Cesar's words broke the unbearable tension, and, with visible relief, people filed out of the room. But David did not move; he simply sat down on the floor and said, "I'm not leaving until I hear the charges against me and until I have a hearing." Cesar ignored him and walked away, speaking in Spanish to the guards. A few people glanced down at David as they passed, but not many. Within a few minutes the room was empty except for David, Sister Denise, and me. Someone had turned out the lights, and the darkness compounded the silence. I heard dogs barking, and a radio sounded faintly in the cool night air.

"David, are you all right," Sister Denise asked softly.

"Yeah, but I think we're in deep shit."

"What do you think they'll do?" My stomach felt the way it had when I told my wife I was in love with another woman. What had begun in such high spirits was ending in horror. My mind wandered crazily, but with its immediate focus on myself. How would I get my lecture notes, which my friends at school had mailed to me so that I could teach the class in labour history? Would the guards be visiting me tonight? Was I in physical danger? How would I get out of here? I wanted to be back on Route 66 headed east across the great desert.

"I think they're going to have me arrested. I think Cesar told Juan Salazar to get the police here."

I said, "Arrested for what? Peacefully protesting this crazy shit? That would be some irony."

"No, for trespassing. You forgot. I don't live here anymore. Cesar threw me out."

"But what about the union's constitution? What about what's fucking right?"

"Cesar couldn't care less. And neither will the cops. Don't you know. Cesar is the law here, and it was pretty apparent that most people don't have a problem with that. But you two ought to get out of here. You haven't been accused of anything."

"No way. I didn't have the nerve to speak out in the meeting. I'm gonna stay. They can arrest me too."

"They won't. Cesar won't want a professor and a nun in jail. I'm just a carpenter, less likely to cause embarrassment you know."

"Maybe I should go talk to Cesar now," said Sister. "Tell him how crazy this is. Maybe this wasn't his idea. Maybe he's calmed down by now. Maybe..."

"Sister, don't you see. This whole thing was planned, by Cesar with his little group of flunkies. This was 'the game.' Juan Reyes and I were just its first victims."

We sat in the dark rooms and talked. La Paz seemed like a tomb, still as a stalking cat in the mountain desert. The only sounds we heard were those of the guards who were piling David's belongings on the walkway in front of his room. At least that's what we thought was happening after we heard a voice commanding, "Take his shit out to the sidewalk."

When the screen door slammed and heavy footsteps sounded on the hallway floor, I knew that David was right. Someone hit the light switch, and by the time my eyes focused, four cops were moving toward David. I made out the words "Mojave Police" on one of their badges.

The largest of the four, a red-faced man with a donut shop belly and a fat ass, said, "You David Young?" He seemed uneasy, as if he grasped the incongruity of arresting a union staff person at union headquarters. He'd busted a few union heads on picket lines and stuck his billy club between the ribs of his share of Mexicans. That's what cops did. But this was something different, new terrain, so to speak, and he didn't have a map.

"That's me. What can I do for ya?"

"Just get up so I can get these cuffs on you. You're under arrest."

"You gonna read me my rights?" The cop tensed and his face turned crimson. One of the others tightened the grip on his billy club and fingered his revolver.

"Don't get smart, buddy. It was your folks called us out here. We ain't never been here before. You must be a real bad actor. Now just get up."

David didn't move and just looked up at the cop with an almost whimsical expression on his face.

"I think he's on a sit-down strike. Ain't that right, buddy?" said one of the fat cop's partners. "We're gonna hafta carry him out. Good thing there's four of us. He's a big fella."

"Suit yourself. By the way, what are the charges?"

"They say you're trespassing. They asked you to leave and you said 'fuck you.'"

"That's a lie, he never said that," I shouted. "And how can he be trespassing? He lives here. I'll show you his room."

"That's not what they say. You got proof you live here. A lease or something."

"What do you think?" David said. "Look, just carry me out of here and get it over with. That's what you're here for. You got TV at your jail?"

"You're such a wise ass, buddy, maybe we'll just...."

"Shut up, Joe," spit the big cop, glaring at us. "Yeah, big guy, we got all the amenities of home. You'll see." He looked at his men and said, "Grab him." Then they carried him out. We followed them to the police car and watched as they shoved him in the middle of the back seat and drove away.

"Sister, I'm getting the hell out of here, now. I'm packing my stuff and I'll drive up to Mojave and try to bail David out of jail. What about you?"

"I have to stay. I'll try to put David's things in my room."

I don't have a very clear memory of the next few days. I did bail David out of jail. One of our friends, Leila, the union organizer who was negotiating with Mr. Fontin in Oxnard, called her parents in San Jose and made arrangements for David to stay with them for a while. I drove him there and stayed the night. Leila's parents were old left Communists, appalled that their daughter had converted to Catholicism, the better to serve the campesinos. The next morning, I headed south and then east toward home.

The Grapes of Wrath was published in 1939. A lot has changed since then; working people began to make a fairly good living, buying good cars and houses and sending their kids to college. But for farm workers the changes haven't been so great. They're still dirt poor. They're still sickly, from bad food, from pesticides, from fouled water. They still don't often live past fifty. And their kids still don't go to school. Their skin colors change, but their lives don't. And what's true here is true everywhere in the world where the big growers own the land. Money is what they want, money in a ceaseless and growing flow, and the way to get it is to have a large reserve army of people without land whose only choice is to harvest the crops for nothing or die. The big growers will do whatever they have to do, including kill people, to ensure the existence of the landless masses. And this is true in the United States, in Mexico, in El Salvador, in the Philippines, in Indonesia, everywhere the land and its bounty have become merely things to buy and sell.

But everywhere the big growers enslave people, some of the people catch on. Some of them figure it out themselves, and some of them get help from the few outsiders who care. They come to understand why they are poor while the bosses are rich. It's a simple thing really, but hard to learn, because the whole of the power of all of the forces that run a society—the owners, the presses, the schools, the churches, the government—have blanketed the people with a heavy weight of lies. Of course, it's a dangerous thing too; in most parts of the world, you'll risk your life to learn it. Yet still some do learn the great truth: that profits and poverty, profits and land-lessness go together. Just like winter and snow in the mountains: where there is one, there is the other. And these people, when they learn the truth, have to act on it. They have to tell others, and then they and the others and the outsiders are transformed. They begin to form study groups, base communities, co-ops, credit unions, labour unions. They meet, they march, they strike, they form armies and they fight to get the land back, to make a decent wage, to live a life of dignity. The big people don't like this, and they torture and kill and bribe and lie to stop it. Most times it stops, but sometimes the poor people win and, when they do, they leave a lesson for those who follow, those who must finally make the land and all of the earth's wealth the equal property of all.

Cesar was one of the people who caught on and then did something about it. What he did was wonderful, magnificent really. He built a union where none had ever been able to exist. He gave people a vision, and the vision made them do things they'd never been able to do before. Mute people gained voices and spread the word across the land. We are poor, but we know why, we know what to do, and we're going to do it. Up and down the valley, they formed their unions and won their contracts, and the growers took heed and were afraid.

But any movement of the poor is a fragile thing; it will be beset by demons from without and within. The external enemies are well-known, constant irritants and often overwhelmingly powerful. Those inside the union are more subtle, yet nearly as destructive: leaders have big and conflicting egos, gender and racial tensions are hard to overcome, people have honest differences about goals and strategies, and it is enormously difficult to create the selfless bureaucracy that alone will ensure the movement's continuity. Cesar learned how to get power and to use it effectively to combat the union's external foes, but such power was also used inside to solidify his personal hold on the movement. As he did this, he came to see the movement as his movement, to shape as he pleased. Anyone inside opposed to him was branded as an outside enemy and excised from the union. His movement was not strong enough to contain him, and the results were like those I have described above. In the years since then, things have gotten worse. Nearly every officer, organizer, and lawyer has been purged or has quit. Most of the membership drifted away, because the union could not keep them under contract with the growers and would not tolerate rank-and-file criticism of Cesar. In 1995, Cesar died at the age of sixty-six. His son-in-law was made union president, and his children now preside over a host of business enterprises funded by government grants and money raised through mass mailings. Cesar's union has become a racket, paying high salaries to its officers while the mass of farm workers still starve. In the end, it seems that a proletarian dictator is no better than any other.

IV.
Alienation and Redemption

V.I. Lenin and Father Roderick

NON-FICTION

I have just given the first examination of the semester. The results are poor, and I am upset. I return the tests and begin my
standard pep talk. I tell them that the reason their grades are
low is because they made inadequate preparation. They missed
too many classes; on most Fridays, more people are absent than
in attendance. They do not know how to take notes. Sometimes
students leave their notebooks behind after class, and when I
notice, I read them. I am surprised how often the notebook
has no name on it. The notes themselves make for depressing
reading. An entire week of complicated and well-thought-out
lectures has been reduced to a single page of semi-coherent
jottings. The only interesting items are the messages sent by
friends to one another, and even these are juvenile and poorly
written. I can imagine a chronic absentee copying these notes
and further reducing them to three or four sentences. Perhaps
if this student lends the copied notes to another and this student to still another, my lectures will eventually be reduced to
a single word. If I knew in advance what this word was, I could
just shout it out at the beginning of class and end things there.

As I warm to my task, I continue to harp about the notes.
Students come up after class and question my grading with

the explanation that what they had written was what they had in their notes. I say that their notes are theirs, not mine, and what they have in them and what I said may be two different things. Once, I was lecturing about the workings of a capitalist economy according to Karl Marx. Marx tells us that our economic system is based upon the "accumulation of capital," the process in which employers exploit their workers to make profits, which are then plowed back into the business so that it can expand in the face of stern competition. Marx uses the story from the Old Testament in which Moses receives the stone tablets from God, on which are written the commandments the Jews must obey. For Capitalists, Marx says, "Accumulate! Accumulate! That is Moses and the prophets." This is such a famous phrase and so well sums up the behavior of business firms that I repeated it a dozen times. As I said it, I wrote it on the blackboard. But because it is physically painful for me to write, I sometimes did not write out the word "Accumulate" and just wrote the letter A. On the final test of the semester, I had a list of simple fill-in questions. One of them, worth two points, said, "_____, _____! That is Moses and the prophets." All that the student had to do was write the word "Accumulate" two times on the appropriate spaces. As students turned in their exams, I started to mark them. I noticed that a number of students had answered this fill-in by writing the letter A twice. This began to infuriate me, so when I noticed that the student who had just handed in her exam had done this, I called her back to my desk before she left the room. I pointed to the two As and asked, "What is this?" She looked and without missing a beat told me, "That's what I have in my notes."

I rant on about preparation. Preparation must be ongoing, I say. I appeal to the athletically inclined. Can you become a good basketball player or wrestler without practicing? You learn how to learn by practicing, by reading as much as you can, by thinking about what you have read, by writing.

Preparation must also be thorough; everything must be learned. Students will sometimes advise me that they are going to miss an upcoming class. They ask, "Will you be covering anything important today." Yes, today and every day. Or they will ask, "Do we have to read the parts of the textbook assigned but not covered in class?" Yes, I chose the book to complement the lectures not substitute for them. Why would I come to class if I had nothing to say? Why would I pick a book I thought was unimportant?

By this time the students are getting angry with me. No one cares much for criticism, no matter how true, and especially if the critic's voice is, perhaps unintentionally, tinged with sarcasm. So, to diffuse their hostility and to make my points less abstractly, I tell them two stories, one about Lenin and one about my old teacher, Father Roderick. Lenin is a favorite of mine, a man of iron will and determination, who once said that he could not listen to Beethoven's Appassionata Sonata because it made you want to hug people when what you needed to do was crack them over the head. Nowadays, I have to identify the great Russian revolutionary. Even before the collapse of the Soviet Union, I had a student write on an examination in a Comparative Economics Systems class that the Bolshevik revolution took place in 1967! In any case, I told my students, Lenin had a facility for languages, which he studied during his years in exile and in prison. An admirer asked him how he approached learning a language. Lenin replied that it was simple. First, you learned all of the nouns. Then you learned all of the verbs. Finally, you learned all of the rules of grammar. Just learn everything, and you'll have it. No tricks. No shortcuts. Just hard work.

Father Roderick gets a longer story. He was my first college history teacher. Few students liked him. Not only was he an impossibly hard grader, but he was also extraordinarily boring. College folklore had it that he had fallen asleep during one of his own lectures. I can still see him pointing with

a yardstick at a map of Europe and droning out in his mono-
tone, "By this time, Spain was a third-rate power," a phrase he
repeated at least twenty times during the term, covering a period of about three centuries. As I am talking to my class, I begin to daydream about those classes from so long ago. There
was something about Father Roderick that I liked. Maybe
it was because he seemed oblivious to his inadequacies as a
teacher. He never seemed to notice our numbed looks, and
he never reacted to the audible groans that emanated from us
at least once in every class. Perhaps it was because, at a fac-
ulty-student "tea" one afternoon, he told me that Eisenhower
had been a lousy president. Father Rod was a liberal, and that
was all right with me. As was the fact that he was a sports fan.
He had been the school's athletic director, though not a good
one, having forgotten to pay the baseball team's tournament
fee the one year the team had been invited to play. He used
to look wistfully over the athletic fields, dressed in his monk's
robes, saying his afternoon prayers.

I explain that Father Rod's tests were devilishly difficult.
They consisted of three parts. Part One was a long match-
ing exercise in which all of the terms were so obscure that it
was not unusual for some students to recognize not a single
one of them. Some of the items were drawn from textbook
footnotes and picture captions. Section Two consisted of the
"Threes"; we would be asked to give three reasons for this,
or to name three of these, and so forth. Father Rod was en-
amoured with threes, as I suppose all priests are. Part Three
required us to write a five hundred-word essay in answer to a
question breathtaking in its generality. One went something
like this: "Discuss the political, social, cultural, and economic
aspects of the decline of the Roman Empire." We had fifty
minutes to complete the examination. It was said that Father
Rod had not given an A in a long time. And no wonder. You
needed 90 percent for an A, and given that you were bound
to lose at least seven to ten points on the essay, you had no

chance for one. Plus, he never rounded a grade up. If you scored 89.9 percent, you got a B. In my first class, I got a B, missing an A by a fraction of a point. I was so disgusted that I became determined to get an A the following term. In fact, I achieved the unprecedented distinction of earning three As in his classes, unprecedented, no doubt, because I am certain that no one ever took four of his classes.

I tell my class about how I succeeded. I explain that I had decided upon a Leninist strategy. Before each test, I rewrote all of my lecture notes, in complete sentences and with insights gathered from the readings. The act of writing the notes helped me understand the material much better. Next, I took the notes and the textbook and made a list of every name, date, and important term in them, including those in the footnotes and picture captions. I then wrote a definition for each of these, a time-consuming task since I might have several hundred entries. But again the act of constructing the definitions greatly aided the learning. I combed through the notes and book one more time, recording every possible "three" I could find, in preparation for Father's obsession with the Trinity. And last, I made a short list of possible essay questions and wrote out at least an outline answer for each one. Now I was ready.

My strategy worked. I got an A, something like 97 percent. As news of this spread, classmates began to ask me for help in boosting their grades. Before the next exam and for the next two semesters, students would gather in a dormitory study room and take notes while I lectured from my preparatory materials. Everyone paid attention, because I now knew what would be on Father Roderick's tests, and my lectures would probably be the difference between a good and a bad grade for my listeners. No one dared interfere with my presentation lest he be shouted down by the others: "Let Mike talk. He has the key to the course."

By the end of the class, at least the students are smiling. Perhaps a few leave the room with a new resolve. It always seems that the grades improve on the next examination. But most likely it is I who have learned the most. I have put what I learned from Lenin and Father Roderick to work in my teaching. I enter class well prepared. I have come to know the material so fluently that I no longer need notes. I can talk for any length of time about a wide variety of subjects. I can teach in large lecture halls to two hundred students or in small seminars. I can do most of the classroom work myself or involve the students in projects of self-learning and discussion. I have had classes in my office, in my living room, in dormitory rooms, and outdoors. I can handle any question, and I can improvise on something I've read in the newspaper or seen on television or that simply pops into my mind while I am talking. I have invented hundreds of examples, and I have a reservoir of dozens of stories and anecdotes to clarify and simplify the subject matter. To give myself credibility I have done work in my teaching areas. I have done economic consulting for attorneys; I have been a labour arbitrator; I have helped to organize unions; I have been a negotiator; and I have written widely on topics related to what I teach. I have taught more than twenty different courses, from Statistics to the Political Economy of Latin America.

For years, I got the biggest kick out of teaching. It seemed an ideal job, one in which I had about as much control as this economic system can tolerate. I enjoyed putting the lectures together and dramatizing them every day in front of the classes. I felt that I was performing a useful and necessary social task, educating young people about the reality of our society and hopefully giving them a more critical outlook than they had ever had. They could take what I taught them and go out and do good deeds and make the world a better place.

Over the years, however, my love affair with teaching faded and finally ended. I do not give my post-test pep talk very often, and the skilled work of preparing the lectures seems wasted effort. The theatricality of the actual teaching has become rote, something I do because I need a paycheck. I still do it better than most, but then, in my experience, most professors are pretty inept. I have tried to figure out why I have lost interest in my job. The students are a big part of it. Their past "mis-education" and total absorption in consumer culture have made most of them incapable of critical thinking. They want instant gratification and cannot be bothered with the work of learning. College, like high school, is just another hoop they have to jump through to get a job that will pay enough money to keep them in cars, houses, VCRs, cell phones, and all the trappings of middle-class living. Most of my students are products of the suburban life and do not know enough or care to learn enough to be interesting to me. I still get some kids who yearn for knowledge and some poor adults who know now that it is important to educate oneself. But these few stand out like sore thumbs, and the other students look at them when they ask and answer questions as if they were creatures from outer space. I do what I can for them, but this does not give me the satisfaction it once did.

I don't mean to disparage the students; they are only partly responsible for being what they are, and there is no point laying all of the blame on them. But still I have to face them every day, and it is not a pleasant experience. There is no longer a mass movement on the campuses to give me hope that what I am doing has social significance. Reagan and his successors have won as far as I can tell. They have made the universities in their own image and likeness, businesses intent on satisfying the customers. As I saw this happening—the overlap of higher education and business, the proliferation of mindless majors like business administration, the exclusion of the poor, the mendacity and self-promotion of teachers and administrators, the dumbing-down of the curriculum—I decided to put my energies elsewhere. I'm sure that there are schools where it is still possible to believe that college teaching is something special. Mine is just not one of them. Luckily for me, what I learned from Lenin and Father Roderick is useful in any work. Too bad my students cannot be made to see this.

Whenever I get despondent about work, my wife tells me that I have had an impact on hundreds of students. If I am particularly irritable, I say, "I doubt it." Then I'll get an email from someone thanking me for classes I taught long ago. I published a book in 1994 in which I acknowledged Father Roderick. I knew he would never see it, so one afternoon we drove to my old college to visit him. I didn't know if he was still alive, but someone in the library said that he was retired and living in the monastery. We found him in his spare monk's room. He didn't remember me, but he was happy that I had remembered him. He said that he had been happiest when he was out of the college and serving as a parish priest. He missed driving a car. Not long after, he died. Maybe, in inadvertent honour of his memory, a few of my students have learned the method I learned when he was my teacher.

The Division Chair

NON-FICTION

We spent too much time in bars drinking, talking, and plotting. He was my best friend, a large and gregarious man of liberal tendencies. To his wife's consternation, he was always challenging the college to do the right thing, whether it was to recruit more minority and foreign students, pay attention to the low salaries of the faculty, end the undemocratic system of promotion and tenure, or address the exploitation of student athletes. Unfairness offended him. I got him interested in labour questions and tried to push his thinking in a more radical direction. It didn't take much pushing. In most respects we were different. I was shy and did not make friends easily; he craved company and had a wide circle of acquaintances. He grew up in a wealthy town and went to an Ivy League college, as did most of his friends, though he did not come from a rich family. His mother grew up poor in an Irish neighborhood in Boston and his father was a Scottish immigrant, who had immigrated to the United States with his machinist father and eventually become a successful accountant.

He was my steadfast ally in the first attempt to unionize the faculty and had championed every attempt by workers on campus to unionize or otherwise fight against our employer.

We caused so much trouble in our first few years at the college that new faculty were told by the dean to avoid us if they wanted their careers to prosper. We had strong supporters, especially those whose own causes we had espoused; we also had enemies, not just in the administration, but also among those teachers whose little fiefdoms we had threatened and among those who could not stomach our politics. For a long time, references to us were always made in the plural "Mike and Bruce said this" or "Bruce and Mike did that" We were disparaged with comments like "What's in this for them?" implying that we must have ulterior motives for what we were doing.

After the first two defeats of the faculty union, we dealt with our demoralization by turning our attention toward local issues, ones we could affect by on-campus agitations. For years the campus had been run in a paternalistic fashion by the deans and certain senior and favoured faculty. We had fought to have a real faculty senate, an organization, typical in colleges, that advises the administration on issues such as the allocation of space on campus and criteria for promotion and tenure. It was a poor substitute for a union, but it offered a forum for faculty complaints and suggestions. We could use faculty senate meetings to raise important social issues, such as university investments in apartheid South Africa or administrative indifference to affirmative action. The dean and the president took umbrage at these political uses of the senate, and we had many confrontations. We had to use some care in this, however, because on any given issue there would be faculty lackeys who could not wait to let the bosses know that they were loyal subjects. One colleague said irritably, after I said that a statement of the dean was the stupidest thing I had ever heard, "You must show the dean some respect." Somehow I cannot imagine one of my father's buddies saying something like that about a foreman.

Our school was divided academically into divisions, one for each broad area of study: social sciences, education, humanities, natural sciences, and engineering. The heads of each division were chosen unilaterally by the dean and president and served indefinitely, until they retired, resigned, or were replaced. The division chairs had power; they made your salary recommendation and they could cause you to be denied contract renewal or tenure. Since they owed their position to the dean, they were by necessity, and usually by temperament, allied firmly with the administration. Our chairman was a long-time faculty member, a local man who had made good, working himself up from the working class to become a professor. Unlike me, however, he had tied his tail to the kite of the town's movers and shakers, always going along with authority and promoting himself at the same time. He wasn't an evil person; he had a well-deserved reputation as a dedicated teacher, and with students he was generous with his time. He treated those under him with an old-fashioned paternalism, calling the secretaries "doll" and acting as if the youngest teachers were his children. Bruce and I bristled at this. I once told him that I already had a father and did not need another one. He took our opposition personally and accused us of "stirring up the pot," causing trouble for its own sake.

We knew that we could not force the administration to replace our chairman; he was too entrenched. But he was getting old and would retire soon. We wanted to be sure that his replacement would be more to our liking, so we began to organize to get what we wanted. We decided that the best course would be to make an issue of the way division chairs were selected. We argued that the faculty should decide who their chair would be; this was the democratic way and would ensure a smoother operation of each division. In addition, the chair should serve a limited term, no more than five years. Then the chair would know that he or she would return to the faculty and would, therefore, be less likely to make arbitrary decisions. Finally, the chairs would have to be subject to periodic faculty reviews. We proposed that a faculty senate committee be established to study this matter and make a formal set of recommendations.

There was great enthusiasm for our motion, and a committee was duly formed. Over the next year, the committee met and hammered out a resolution. The end result was not exactly what we wanted, but it was a great improvement over the status quo. The faculty endorsed it nearly unanimously, and it was sent to the administration for approval. The dean and the president were appalled by this attempt to undermine their authority and promptly ignored it and stonewalled our efforts to get them to act. After another year, we got the senate to call a special meeting with the president to discuss the proposal. The room was packed, and we were loaded for bear. The president, a pleasant but not overly intellectual man, began to talk, in his usual indirect way, about the school's administrative structure, but we soon interrupted him.

"What was there about our proposal to which he objected?"

"Did he believe that the faculty should not have the primary responsibility in selecting a division chair?"

He hemmed and hawed. He was in a bind and knew it. Colleges operate under the fiction that there is a system of shared governance between the teachers and the administration. Teachers do get to make certain recommendations, but authority lies with the Board of Trustees, dominated by the business community. Usually there are enough teachers who believe the hype about faculty input, but at this meeting, too many of us knew better. We wouldn't let up and badgered the president into a corner. In a rare display of anger, he finally said that he, and he alone, appointed the chairs and that was the way it was whether we liked it or not. For once, the power of the boss was made transparent.

After the meeting, the president realized his mistake, and the administration did present us with a counter-proposal. It granted some of our demands but watered them down and kept intact the president's final power of determination. He and the dean calculated that the teachers, with little stomach for long-term confrontation, would back down and take the compromise. They were right. But at least we now had a document that could help us determine who our own chair would be.

Our division chair soon announced his retirement. This set us into action. We let it be known that Bruce, himself, wanted the job, and we began to line up support for him. Bruce had never been as excited about teaching as I had been. He wanted something more. He had administrative experience outside the university, and he had a talent for getting things done and in getting along with people of diverse temperaments. He used to love to watch the college's buildings being constructed, and he took a keen interest in the planning of them. I always said that he would have made a great construction supervisor. He had many friends in the division, and there did not appear to be any viable challengers. We huddled over our beers at our favorite bar and worked out our campaign.

The only person who might challenge us was another professor who had spent his career ingratiating himself with the current chair and the administration. He exuded an air of superiority and had an unwarranted reputation as a scholar and teacher. He was obsessed with order and devoted to the idea of hierarchy, a place for everything and everything in its place. He could not stand, to the point of physical sickness, any disorder, even going to the extreme of writing students' names on their own examination booklets. Despite his favor with the administration, he was disliked by the faculty. We couldn't stand his elitism, his long-winded and tedious memos, his disdain for anyone not above him in the school's hierarchy, his willingness to stab his colleagues in the back, and his coldness and inability to show normal emotions. I remember the headache we gave the old chairman at this professor's promotion review meeting. We went around the room and every person had something negative to say about him. There was no chance he would be selected chair if the faculty had anything to say about it.

I pride myself on understanding the behavior of employers but, like most people, I want to believe that the truth will win out in the end and in any contest the participants will play fairly. Hope springs eternal. This belief proved naive. Soon after Bruce announced his candidacy, the administration went to work. A "compromise" candidate suddenly appeared, a younger teacher and one of the few allied with both the old chair and the old chair's protégé. This man had the same characteristics as his more reviled colleague, but he had the ability to suppress these in public and come across as sincere and friendly. He was presented by supporters as running not out of personal ambition but to give us a choice for chair. In reality, he had no supporters and had instead been asked by the dean in secrecy to run against Bruce.

We still believed that we would win, because Bruce was the more qualified person, and his rival was so clearly the administration's candidate. But behind the scene, our enemies were at work. They began to spread rumors about us: We only wanted power. We were openly ambitious. Bruce had a drinking problem. Bruce was too emotional, something undesirable in a professor, who must show neutrality in the classroom. The most vulnerable teachers in the division were pressured to vote against Bruce. I overheard the old chair and the protégé agreeing that a teacher who had mental problems and was near the point of emotional collapse should be cornered and more or less ordered to vote for the compromise candidate. This poor fellow later came into Bruce's office in tears, telling him how he had been browbeaten. My radicalism was singled out. If Bruce were chosen, that communist Yates would be the real chair. Occasionally, I overreacted to these charges, and this, it was argued, was not appropriate behavior and showed our immaturity.

This misinformation campaign began to work. Teachers were made to feel that Bruce and I were the cause of the tension in the division, tension that would only worsen if he were elected. It was much the same strategy as the university employed to defeat the teachers' union. Teachers do not usually have the courage to stand up to such turmoil, to understand its roots and fight for the changes necessary to overcome it. They want to return to the comfort of their isolated offices and classrooms. I began to notice that teachers who were personal friends and strong initial supporters would not publicly endorse Bruce or campaign for him. They began to say that maybe either person would be acceptable. They said that maybe Bruce would be better off emotionally if he did not get the job. After all, there was some truth, they hinted, to the administration's characterization of Bruce's personality. There was one teacher, in particular, much respected in the division, upon whom I had counted to openly endorse Bruce. But when I asked her, she hedged.

The dean devised a complex ballot to obtain faculty sentiment. One of the choices on the ballot was "Both candidates are acceptable." This was ingenious because it gave the teachers a way out. They could check this box and tell themselves that they had not voted against Bruce. In the end, Bruce actually got one more favorable vote than his rival, but most people had stated that both were acceptable. This was all that the dean needed to see. He held that Bruce had been defeated, and our carefully laid plans went for naught.

Our friendship suffered a blow in all of this. Bruce blamed me in part for his defeat. If only I had not been so confrontational, perhaps we would have won. Today, I am sure he never had a chance to begin with. Power only respects equal or greater power, and we did not have enough of it. Only an organized power, like a union, has a chance to defeat the enemy of the workers. And before a union can win, the workers have to understand what they are and have the courage to do something about it. Some college teachers have seen the light, especially those most exploited: graduate students and part-timers. But ordinary, tenured faculty members have not.

Two Sick Children

NON-FICTION

Art was one of my colleagues. We hired him to replace a teacher who had taken another job. Art was a friendly guy, although he was difficult to talk to. You'd strike up a conversation, and then suddenly it seemed to end. Probably if I had taken the trouble to know him better, we'd have had better rapport. The times we socialized together, the talk moved more freely, perhaps because a few drinks helped to ease his shyness. Art was a good teacher; he worked hard to learn more about economics and prepare new materials for his classes. He was adept with computers and had cleverly integrated their use into the classroom. He got upset like the rest of us that most of his students were business majors without much interest in the difficult subject matter of economics. I felt fortunate that he was not a libertarian or conservative like so many economists. He and his wife, who also taught at our college, were liberals and not afraid to stand up for what they believed.

When Art began to teach, he had some problems, as most new teachers do. He had earned his PhD from an Ivy League school, but not in economics. He had also taken course credits toward an MBA and had completed all but his dissertation in economics. He then taught abroad for a while. When he returned to the United States, we hired him. His students in Iran had been highly motivated and knowledgeable. For the most part, this was not true in his new school. When he used materials that had been successful with students overseas, he assumed that they would work with our students. Compounding his difficulties was the fact that he was an "egghead," a person who loved ideas, who read omnivorously, and assumed that students were like him. His wife once told me that he would walk around their apartment with his infant daughter on one arm while reading the *Wealth of Nations*, which he was holding in the other hand. A person like this might be much endeared by the novelists of academic life, but he was bound to have trouble with our often barely literate clientele. Students complained that he was too "abstract" and couldn't get the material across. Because even the good students were protesting, our division chairman asked me, the current department head, to do something. He set up a meeting in the library at which I could discuss Art's classes with the students. The meeting was set for a Saturday morning, and all that preceding week I was anxious. This was the last thing I wanted to do, meet with hostile students on my day off. What would I tell them? I sympathized with Art more than with them. I was sure that in due time, he would "come down to their level" like the rest of us and become a good teacher.

That Saturday morning was memorable. About a dozen students were waiting for me, and they started right in on poor Art. I kept asking myself, why did I come here? I had no idea what to tell them, and what I did say sounded ridiculous. I actually said that they should feel free to sit in on another professor's classes to make up for what they were not getting from Art. When I said this, the student sitting across from me, a mother with four children, exploded. She wasn't about to waste her time going to yet another class. What kind of suggestion was that? I mumbled something and got out of there as fast as I could.

Art did get better. Within a year or two after my meeting with the students, he was getting excellent reviews on his student evaluations. He was teaching a wide range of courses and was developing expertise in international economics and finance. Some of the students who had complained the loudest in the library meeting were now praising him for his interesting lectures and willingness to tutor them when they had difficulties. He had some writing projects underway and was participating in division and college affairs. He came up for contract renewal at the end of his second year and was renewed. The faculty committee and the division chair noted his teaching progress. The only reservation noted was his lack of a PhD in economics, and it was stated that the division expected him to have this degree by the time he came up for tenure, at the end of his fifth year.

As the tenure review approached, Art had not yet finished his degree. This worried me, but I began to think that this should not make any difference. He had done all of the course work, and, besides, he already had a doctorate in history from a fine school. As I saw it, a degree in history was more difficult to get than one in economics. A history degree requires that the student do detailed research in primary documents at various libraries, while one in economics demands only that the candidate test a narrow hypothesis within the framework of the neoclassical theory. The writing of a thesis is a good exercise in discipline and it helps a person to think through a subject, but these are benefits that accrue to the writing of a dissertation in any field. Art had taken the course work in economics necessary for a degree, and he had been teaching satisfactorily for five years. What would writing a second dissertation do for him or his students?

However, my way of seeing this was not shared by most of the other tenured teachers in the division. They wanted to see the thesis. Some said that Art had promised to do it, and failure to do what he had said he would do was a character flaw.

The inability to produce the economics PhD was linked to other alleged inadequacies. Art was always late with his class schedules and yearly self-evaluations. I suspected that some division members saw Art as physically soft and intellectually undisciplined and these, in themselves, were enough to deny Art a permanent position.

Some of Art's supporters met with him to discuss the upcoming tenure review. One of us had an idea. Though Art had never mentioned it in connection with his work, his family was undergoing a series of ghastly traumas. Art and his wife had two children, and both of them had been gravely ill. One was diagnosed with a brain tumor. Initial tests showed it to be malignant, which meant that the youngster would die. Later diagnostics would show this to be incorrect, and surgery would remove the benign tumor and give the child a new lease on life. But what must Art have felt, believing that his child would perish? How unimportant a second PhD must have seemed by comparison, and this was even more the case in a division in which no one in the large business department had a PhD. What nightmare could cause more suffering than the death of your child? Compounding his family's woes was the illness of his other child, who had a cancer of the skin and had to undergo extended medical treatment. Between trips to the doctor's office, journeys to distant clinics, and constant worry, it is amazing that Art could perform so well as a teacher. It was hard to see how he could have the time or energy to write another dissertation. As I reflected on this, I got angry. We should never have demanded the second PhD in the first place. We had placed an intolerable burden on this man, and now we were accusing him of being a liar.

The university had a policy that stated that a teacher could move out of the tenure stream for up to two years if he or she had a compelling argument for needing more time to prepare for the tenure review. Art's case seemed a natural for this exception. Art did not want to take this option, but with some prodding, he agreed to it. He put in a formal proposal to be removed from the tenure stream for one year to give him time to finish his degree. Now all we had to do was convince the tenured teachers to recommend this to the administration. I thought that this would be easy. It was only a year, and if Art failed to get close to his degree within the year, we could deny him tenure then. We took no risks.

Sixteen faculty members plus the division chair (the man who had defeated Bruce) came to the meeting to decide Art's fate. I presented the arguments for a one-year suspension of the tenure stream. What followed shocked me. Right away people suspected a trick, a way for Art to evade his duty to get the degree he had promised. Others pointed out Art's general failings, bringing up his early teaching difficulties and his laxness in meeting deadlines. One person suggested that Art's professional development, meaning research and publications, showed "poor career management." His supporters deflected these criticisms as best they could. We said that many teachers failed to meet deadlines, that few of us had been good "career managers," that Art was now a good teacher, that his professional development was at least average for the division. His critics then shifted tactics and started to talk about principles. One person worried about setting a bad precedent for future tenure cases. At this I exploded. "How many teachers with two children with cancer do you think we will have in the future?" We went back and forth on the issue of precedent until one faculty member said something astounding. This professor said that Art's wife no doubt did most of the child care, so the fact that his children were ill did not unduly impose upon him. I thought that this was the most callous remark I had ever heard. Was this professor actually saying that men don't care about their children, and so it follows that nothing about their children should have any bearing on their work? So many emotions swirled through me: fury, disgust, hate. With what little self-control I had left, I suggested that we ought to vote and get this over with.

The voting was by secret ballot. We cast our votes and the chair of the committee counted them. The vote was eight for and eight against Art's petition to be removed for one year from the tenure stream. A tie vote loses, and Art's request was denied. I left the room beaten down by "man's inhumanity to his fellow man." My colleagues had said to Art: "Your kids' sickness be damned. You did not do your job. Be gone! It's a worse crime to not do what you said you would do than to neglect your children." I never felt the same about my job after this meeting.

Ironically, this story had a happy ending. Art's children recovered. And Art did get tenure. After the refusal to extend his apprenticeship, we decided to simply present him for tenure "as is." Perhaps feeling shame over what they had done or because they believed that he would be turned down by the administration, the committee voted to recommend tenure. The division chairman refused to go along and mounted a campaign to deny tenure. He wrote a disingenuous letter announcing his disagreement with the committee. He made phone calls to Art's university to try to uncover evidence that Art had intentionally misled us about his dissertation progress. He assiduously went through Art's professional development, noting weaknesses, including grammatical errors. He presented his report to the college-wide tenure committee, comprising representatives from each of the divisions. Art chose me to be his advocate, an option available when a tenure recommendation from the faculty was not endorsed by the division chair.

The division chair was unhappy to see me. He knew that I thought he had a personal vendetta against Art and was not above stretching the truth, and he knew that I would use this meeting not only to defend Art but to make public his sordid role in this.

After the chair made his case, he left the room and I began to fight for Art's tenure. I answered all of the chair's charges and tried to answer the questions of those who thought that perhaps Art should not get tenure. The meeting lasted two hours, but we got a majority to vote in Art's favor. The recommendation went to the dean and then to the president. The chair and the old chair's protégé lobbied them to deny Art his job. I lobbied too. I do not know why exactly, but the dean and the president decided to give Art tenure.

Teaching the Workers

NON-FICTION

I developed my teaching philosophy from the famous dictum of Karl Marx: "The philosophers of the world have only interpreted the world in various ways; the point is to change it." As I came to see it, only the economics of Marx, radical economics, uncovered the inner workings of our economy and showed why and how this system had to be transcended if human beings were to liberate themselves, that is, gain control over their labour. I had to incorporate these ideas into my own classes; I had to make them the foundations of my work.

The question was how to do this, how to show students the superior insights of Marxian economics in classes that had always been taught from the traditional or neoclassical perspective—taught, in fact, as if the neoclassical theory developed by Adam Smith and his progeny was the gospel truth. This proved to be a difficult endeavor. My colleagues expected that I would teach students the "principles" of economics: that people act selfishly and independently of one another, that this selfishness generates socially desirable outcomes, and that capitalism is a maximally efficient system. Had I refused to do this and taught only Marx's theory of capital accumulation, I could not have kept my job. Right-wing extremists like Rush

Limbaugh and Newt Gingrich would have us believe that the colleges are hotbeds of radicalism, but this is not so. Radical thought gained greater legitimacy during the 1960s and 1970s, but in most places the nation's predominant ideology, fervent anti-communism, was so strong that radical thought (Marxism in particular) was dismissed out of hand as propaganda. If I mentioned Marx in a favorable light, I was branded a communist. Once, when a guest speaker asked one of our history professors why I had criticized his remarks so strongly, she just said, "Oh, don't bother with him, he's a Marxist."

Nearly all of my students were hostile to radical perspectives, having been taught since birth that such views were un-American. Sometimes I could feel their animosity, especially when I pointed out the many things they did not know about our country's unsavoury relationships with the rest of the world.

My own timidity also made it difficult for me to advocate radical ideas. The neoclassical way of thinking has a strong hold on those who have taken the time to learn it. It is elegant, precise, mathematical. No other social science has anything like it; the most mediocre economist feels superior to the best sociologist. Sometimes I was afraid that the neoclassical theory would prove itself capable of answering the questions that its failure to address had led me to look elsewhere in the first place. I gave it a legitimacy that it didn't deserve and spent too much time talking about it in my classes.

So I proceeded in a cautious manner. First, I focused on what economists call "market failures." A market failure occurs when the pursuit of self-interest by the participants in the marketplace does not lead to socially desirable results. An example is the inability of a market system to prevent environmental destruction. In a pure market, companies have no incentive to behave in an environmentally responsible way. It pays for them to shift the environmental cost of their production onto others, who suffer higher health costs, foul air, and dirty water.

Since the market does not respond to our need for a livable environment, it is necessary for the government to impose upon the polluters the responsibility to behave in a socially responsible way. Discussions of market failures allowed me to show my students that a market system has to be regulated, by the government, if it is to satisfy human needs. However, this was liberal and not radical advocacy. My growing hostility to capitalism demanded more than a liberal critique.

My next strategy was to pit the neoclassical and the radical theories directly against one another. I pointed out that economists did not agree on what made capitalist economies tick. I explained the neoclassical theory as objectively as possible. I then used the market failures to develop a criticism of the theory, which led directly into a discussion of Marxian economics. Most students could tell that I was a radical economist, but just a few accused me of bias.

I grew unhappy with this comparison approach, although I still used it in my large introductory classes. The neoclassical theory is difficult for students to learn, so I had to spend too much time teaching it, leaving not enough time to teach the radical theory. Therefore, I did two things. I simply stopped teaching the core courses in economics, called micro and macro economics. This avoided conflict with my neoclassical colleagues and freed me to develop new courses. I was able to do this because I now had tenure and was the senior teacher in my division. I taught the Political Economy of Latin America, a subject amenable to a radical analysis and one considered so unimportant by my fellow economists that they did not complain that I taught it from a radical perspective. I was aided by the fact that most Latin American economists are more open to radical theories than their North American counterparts. I also developed a set of courses in labour relations as a way to attract unsuspecting business majors to my courses. I built these courses on the supposition that there is an inherent conflict between employees and their employers. This conflict is rooted in the nature of our economic system, as first explained by Marx. In these classes, the only theoretical constructs employed were those of Marx and his modern adherents. However, while I advocated a radical perspective and hoped that students would adopt it as their own, I did this in such a way that I doubt that many of them knew what I was doing. I borrowed from the neoclassical economists' method: I assumed that my model was correct and proceeded accordingly.

I had some success with my teaching and, until the end of the 1970s, I was relatively happy. But then disillusion set in. In part this was due to the sharp rightward shift in the nation's politics and its repercussions in the colleges and universities. The student revolt of the 1960s generated a counterattack by the leaders of business (who dominate the schools to a degree seldom examined or understood) and government. One result of this was strong pressure on academe to become more career-oriented; soon, business and technical programs proliferated. The collapse of the post-Second World War economic boom created understandable fears among young people, and they were persuaded that they had better view their educations as investments in their "human capital" (as the neoclassical economists say) and major in something practical. It wasn't long before I lost my economics majors to business.

There were other reasons for my dilemma, however. The neoclassical dominance in economics had been shaken, but not seriously challenged, by the student revolt. For example, I could not get another radical economist hired into my department. Instead we hired mostly conservative economists, including two libertarians (extremists as far as classroom advocacy goes but rarely viewed as such). My colleagues campaigned to marginalize my new courses, refusing to count their credits toward the major in economics. The business department eliminated them from a list of acceptable courses in its management major.

The triumph of neoclassical economics was aided by the backsliding of radical economists. Many of them adopted the tenets of postmodernism and rejected Marx's most fundamental insights, which rest on the primacy of class as the factor accounting for the main contours of capitalism. And instead of using the collapse of the Soviet Union as a springboard for an attack on capitalism (whose proponents could no longer use communism as a smokescreen to hides its weaknesses), radical economists moved to the right.

Finally, it became clear to me that advocating radical ideas in my classrooms was not going to help push the society toward greater egalitarianism and more control over the economy by ordinary people. Colleges in the United States have no tradition of radical activity like their counterparts in the rest of the world. Before the 1970s, it is difficult to think of any great radical professors in economics beside Thorstein Veblen. During the 1960s, there was one openly radical tenured professor of economics in the entire nation, Stanford economist Paul Baran. Most faculty identify more with the business and political elites than with working and poor persons. They hesitate to do anything to jeopardize their careers and future consulting work. Most are comfortable with corporate influence, whose growth is hardly likely to encourage critical thinking much less radical advocacy.

I continued to teach as I had before, but I knew that if society's class structure was to radically change, it would only happen if working people saw the need for this to happen. The student radicals of the 1960s opened up the universities, forcing them, for example, to end many of their racist and sexist practices. But they worked on the false assumption that social change could emanate from the colleges and universities. Years of experience taught me that this is untrue. Therefore, I turned my attention outside the classroom. I helped the maintenance and custodial workers form a labour union, and I tried to get the teachers to follow suit.

Most importantly, I began teaching working people directly in a labour studies program run by another college. For twenty-eight years I have been teaching workers. There are many things I enjoy about this. These students are often like the people with whom I grew up; the older students sometimes remind me of my father and his factory workmates. All of them have job experience and so understand work better than my college students. When I talk about the labour law or unemployment, they can bring interesting personal experiences to the discussions. What I teach has immediate practical relevance to them, and I can use this to get them to understand more complex and abstract economic and political ideas. For example, I once taught collective bargaining to a group of men working in a plant that made air conditioners. They had been forced by their international union to make concessions during the term of their collective bargaining agreement. They videotaped the classes and showed the tapes to co-workers. Then they ran a slate of candidates in their local union elections and won office. Using some of the things they had learned in the class, they successfully negotiated the return of the things they had been compelled to concede. One of the new officers went on to get a Masters degree in labour relations and then taught classes in the same program in which I worked. In a real sense, these classes have been catalysts for the rebuilding of long dormant local labour movements. They have raised the class consciousness of many of the students in them.

Although many of my worker students have not graduated from college, they grasp economic theory more quickly and deeply than did my college pupils. This is because the theory has a greater usefulness to them, and they perceive the arguments through the lenses of working people's eyes. Two examples come to mind. In a class in labour economics, we were discussing the differences between the neoclassical and the Keynesian theories of unemployment. After two three-hour classes, one of the students was able to write a prize-winning essay on the subject for his local union newspaper. In a class in labour law, we were examining the Fourth Amendment to the Constitution in the context of employee drug testing. In my college classes, most students take it for granted that employers have the right to randomly drug test employees. They have been so thoroughly brainwashed that they do not think of the issue in terms of civil liberties. The workers, on the other hand, argued vehemently against drug testing under any circumstances. Most of them said that they would refuse, as a matter of principle, to be drug tested. All of this is not to say that my worker students are perfect. Far from it. They have been subjected to the same kind of conservative advocacy from family, media, teachers, and employers to which all of us are exposed. Racism and sexism are recurring problems, although my college students were more racist and sexist than the working men and women I teach.

Teaching workers has been teaching as I envisioned it when I became a teacher: students come to class voluntarily, and even though the classes often run late at night and for three hours, the students enthusiastically participate in their learning and then go out to apply what they have learned to their lives. They appreciate my commitment to teaching; applause and gifts at the end of a course are not uncommon. And I have found that these are students from whom I can learn new things as well. My labour education classes have inspired me to write several books, all of which are aimed at the general working public. Through these books, I have made contact with working class groups around the country and have had the opportunity to give talks, conduct seminars, and help in union-organizing campaigns. I often get calls from working people asking for my help in legal or economic matters. Nothing comparable happened in my college classes.

The best thing about teaching workers is that I do not have to abide by or feel pressured by the canons of academe. I do not have to worry that my students will not know what they are expected to know when they take intermediate economics courses. I do not have to maintain an air of objectivity when I discuss economics. I do not have to say, for example, that economists disagree about how a capitalist economy works; instead, I can say what I believe, forthrightly, that neoclassical economics is the economics of the employing class and that the attempt to make it into something else, a set of universal truths, is propaganda. I can posit a radical explanation of capitalism. This is always well received. This is because it fits with their actual work experiences; it helps them to understand what they are, what forces and persons are responsible for their circumstances, and what they might do to combat them. In the worker classrooms, I can be the advocate I think I should be, openly and without fear.

In the college classroom, I taught the way I did because the college was structured such that a more honest and direct approach was not possible. I teach the workers the way I do because with them it is possible to do so. Academe, by its nature, limits, constrains, absorbs, or punishes direct radicalism. And if it does allow some radical advocacy, it is so far removed from the lives of working people that such advocacy is bound to have little radical social impact. It will not help to transform society into the egalitarian and democratic world I envision. Worker education, on the other hand, offers much greater possibilities, precisely because it is directly connected to the lives of the working class majority, who, in the end, must be the moving force of social transformation.

At the "Wall"

NON-FICTION

Pennsylvania's Western Penitentiary, known to its residents as "The Wall," was a maximum security prison (it has since been closed), sitting along the Ohio River on the far north side of Pittsburgh. The spot is a pretty one, although in the fenced-in former parking lot facing the river, to which the inmates had occasional access, the fence itself was covered with plastic sheeting so that they could not see the water.

I taught classes in economics at this prison for two years on Tuesday evenings. I arrived a little after 6:00 p.m., signed in at the front desk, and presented myself to a guard. I emptied my pockets and took off my belt and shoes if they had any metal on them. The guard checked my bag, and I walked through a metal detector. I had a cushion with me because I couldn't sit on a hard chair without pain. I had to get prior permission from the superintendent's office to bring in this cushion, and it was checked by the guard each time I came for class. After passing through the metal detector and back out again, I went in. Another guard took a filter of some sort and put it into a machine that looked like a miniature dust buster. He ran this over my palms, my jacket pockets, my pants and shirt pockets, and my pants cuffs. Then he removed the filter and put it into another machine that checks for of a wide variety of drugs. A marker visible to a special light was used by the guard to mark my hand. I was given an ID card with my picture on it, and I placed this in a visible place on my shirt or jacket. Then another guard was called by the one at the desk, and he came out to escort me to the school building inside the prison. We awaited the opening of a set of double doors by still another guard, invisible to us. The doors opened and we walked down a hallway to another set of doors that opened into the yard of the prison. We walked a block or so through several gates to the school building, and the guard let me into the classroom.

I awaited the arrival of the students. They were sometimes late, for any number of reasons; prisons have many checks on prisoners and these take time. Not all of the students made every class. Some of them were on various sorts of punishment. One man missed a class because he rebelled when he was not allowed to go to the funeral home to see his dead mother's body. I made small talk with the guards. It was best to keep on their good side as they could make life difficult for me if they wished. If I planned to use a video or a film, I had to let them have it in advance. Before this procedure was implemented, a teacher showed the film *The Battle of Algiers* to a class studying Franz Fanon's *Wretched of the Earth*. This probably would have been prohibited had she had to show the film to the prison administrators first. Generally, you can use any materials you want, but titles referring to persons such as Mumia or Leonard Peltier will probably be confiscated, if not from us then from the inmates.

I never felt unsafe in the prison. However, I did jump the first time the double doors slammed behind me (just like in the movies). And I was nervous about the first class. To do a bad job here was just unthinkable. It was not a credit class. The government took away Pell Grants (financial aid) from the prisoners, and so they could not afford to attend college.

When this happened, the University of Pittsburgh closed the degree program it once had there. A friend of mine, who helps run the current program, did not want to see all non-vocational programs end at the prison, so she and another person started a non-credit certificate program. So far, it has been a great success.

In my first class, I had the students sign the roster sheet and asked them to put down, in addition to their given names, any name they preferred me to use. Some wrote down Muslim names, one an Egyptian name, and some nicknames. So I had Khalifa, Senifer, Heru, Farid Rafiq, Bamoni, Crump, Capone, and Muscles as well as Charlie and Deion. They ranged in age from early twenties to late forties. I did not know why they were in prison. All but one of the students was black (I am white), and it struck me right away that not one of the black students was light-skinned. They did not look like the African American newscasters we see now on television. Not only do black Americans face an abominable discrimination that puts so many in prison, but those with the darkest skin color also face this discrimination most forcefully.

I began the first class by saying something about myself. A student interrupted me and asked if any of my college students had gone on to become CEOs! I replied that I had a former student who was now a rich bond broker on Wall Street but I did not know whether to be proud of this or not. Then I passed out some handouts. I started to talk about capitalism and what I thought were its main features. Then I asked a question about wealth and the discussion began. I can only describe it as a runaway train. We talked about many things, for at least an hour without a stop. Some comments were as sharp as any I have ever heard from a student, some were funny, and some reflected views common on the outside. But all were made seriously, by men wanting to know and to have their voices heard. I was exhilarated in a way seldom so in my regular classes. When I got home I slept fitfully. I kept thinking about the class and I kept seeing the students' faces. I dreamed about them most of the night.

The next class was just like the first. We discussed an article called "Buddhist Economics" by E. F. Schumacher, from his book *Small is Beautiful* and compared the Buddhist concept of Right Livelihood with work and consumption in capitalism. This time we went on for an hour and a half. Then I took a break, but they were back in their seats in a few minutes. I gave a brief lecture about the accumulation of capital. I had Marx's famous letter scheme, M-C-C-M, on the chalkboard, and I explained what each letter meant while they wrote furiously on their notepads. The class ended with me pounding on the table, saying "Accumulate! Accumulate! that is Moses and the Prophets." I had their complete and undivided attention when I said this and then argued that capital will be accumulated whatever the cost, whether it be enslavement, theft, or murder.

During this class, I felt something I have never felt in a class before. I know that this may sound naive, but I felt sitting there with convicts all around me, that we really were brothers. We left the class together after the whistle shrilly blew the signal that they had to return to their cellblocks. We walked down the steps of the classroom building and out into the yard among the general prison population. I looked up at the stars and my heart was filled with a hard sadness.

V.
Pessimism of the Intellect, Optimism of the Will

Removing the Veil

NON-FICTION

The people in these essays and stories, including myself, are embedded in and shaped by what for most of us is an obscured reality. The most important thing to know about this reality is that we live in a capitalist society. Most of us have been taught to believe that such a society is too complex to understand. The average person is ignorant of economics, so much so, politicians and pundits can say preposterous things and never be called to account. The former president of the United States, George W. Bush, can state, without a shred of evidence, that the social security system is soon to be bankrupt, and no one will call him a liar.

They say that appearances are deceiving, and this is true of our capitalist economy. Its operation is not so complex that it cannot be grasped by any person of normal intelligence. The first thing to know is that almost all of what is said by the politicians, television pundits, and mainstream economists is wrong. It is mostly propaganda, and it is put out there to deceive us.

Why would those who should know how the economy works not tell us the truth? One reason is that many of them don't recognize the truth. However, a deeper reason has to do with what really goes on in a capitalist economy. Such an economy is one in which society's productive nonhuman resources—land, raw materials, tools, machines, buildings, and the like—are the private property of a small fraction of the total population. This productive wealth, when combined with human labour, produces the food, clothing, and shelter we all need to survive. It is not hard to see that power will be in the hands of whatever group controls the resources that produce the things we all must have to live. For example, we must have access to the land to get food, but the land is monopolized by a minority of persons.

In a capitalist economy, most people can gain access to the land and other "means of production" in only one way: by selling their ability to work (their "labour power") to the owners of these resources. We offer our labour power to them in exchange for a wage, and we use our pay to buy the things we need.

Anyone who has looked for work knows that a working person does not often face a prospective employer on an equal footing. We know that there are always other workers seeking employment, and, if given a chance, most of them could do as good a job as we could. We do not have to take any particular job, but we must take some job. Given that most of us have no appreciable productive wealth (if we all had such wealth, we would not be living in a capitalist society), we cannot start a business of our own. So we look for work in circumstances best described as many interchangeable workers facing a few employers.

In such conditions, who will have the advantage? Can we suppose that hundreds of thousands of men and women go to work for Wal-Mart eagerly seeking to wear uniforms, sing company songs, smile all day long, and work for low wages without benefits? Or that children of less than ten years of age just can't wait to make bricks and soccer balls twelve hours a day or labour as camel jockeys? To paraphrase Karl Marx, most workers must go hat-in-hand to an employer. They enter the workplace with nothing but their hides and can expect nothing but a hiding.

The unequal relationship between workers and employers is the most important feature of capitalism. An understanding of it is the key to knowing how the system works.

The relationship between those who own the means of production and those who do not defines the class structure of the society. The workers make up the working class, and the employers the capitalist class. Neither class exists by itself but only in its connection to the other.

How does the class structure play itself out in our economy? Workers sell their labour power to an employer for a wage payment. The employer, through its ownership of the business, organizes the way in which the work is done in such a fashion that the employer's domination of this "labour process" is as thoroughgoing as possible. Techniques have been developed by employers over the past three hundred years to control what workers do. Employers have herded workers into factories, where they can be monitored and studied. They have taken skilled labour and divided it into unskilled details, both to lower wages and to deny workers knowledge about how the product is made. They have systematically observed and timed workers to steal their "tricks of the trade" and force them to work just as the management says they should. The list goes on and on. But the ability of employers to control is implicit in their ownership, in their class position.

The purpose of management is to convert the employees' potential to work into the maximum amount of actual work. The employer must be able to get workers to work long and hard enough to produce an output which, when sold, will not only cover the employer's costs (of means of production and labour) but also yield a profit. If the workers themselves controlled production, they might or might not choose to work hard enough to produce a surplus over costs. And if they did, they would control the profits and decide what to do with them. But in capitalism, the product and the profits belong to the employer. Workers are compelled to give up sufficient labour because they are not owners and risk being fired if they do not. Put bluntly, workers have to submit to the exploitation by others of their ability to work.

Why do employers have to exploit workers? In a capitalist economy, each employer attempts to accumulate capital, which means that each capitalist enterprise tries to make as much profit as possible and to grow as much as possible. Everything that a business does is tied to the bottom line; there is no room for sentimentality or charity or altruistic behavior. This is because every employer faces a vicious and unyielding competition from other employers. Should a business not make profit and grow, it will fail. The owner's economic well-being, political power, and social status are tied to the firm's success, so failure exacts a high price. However, success is a matter of compelling workers to give up as much of their labour as possible.

A capitalist economy is expansionary by its nature. Its growth is dependent on the exploitation of workers. However, there is no guarantee that workers will go along with this. While an employer is compelled by market competition to think of workers as paid-for commodities, as objects on par with machines or raw materials, workers do not think of themselves that way. They are human beings and have human needs. They need social interactions, they need love, they need to feel connected to the work they do. It is possible, then, that workers will object to their treatment and try to do something about it.

Workers are the only "active" element in production; only they can threaten the accumulation of capital. In most cases, the only way workers can do this is to act together, to organize collectively. Once employers have subdivided tasks and begun to use mainly unskilled labour, an individual worker can do little but quit to protest his or her work circumstances. And there is no guarantee that at any given time there will not be a surplus of skilled workers, so even they may not be able to mount effective opposition individually. Therefore, controlling the workers means that employers must be able to prevent them from joining and acting together.

Much of the history of capitalism can be told in terms of attempts by employers to prevent or defeat collective actions by their employees. In terms of capital accumulation, nothing is more important. Employers have fired, demoted, and maimed workers; had them arrested; used superior political power to make picketing, strikes, and boycotts illegal; and even murdered workers to prevent them from organizing.

While direct attacks against workers have been of great importance to employers, such actions presume that workers have already developed a sense of common purpose sufficient to engage in threatening conduct. Such a sense of common resolve is called "class consciousness," and it is a necessary condition for challenging the capitalists. If ways can be found to prevent its development, the task of employers is made much simpler.

All employer attempts to stifle class consciousness can be summed up as "ideological warfare," the struggle to win the hearts and minds of the workers. It is fair to say that the system conspires, through the efforts of economic elites and their allies, to convince working men and women that there is no such thing as class, and that those who say there is are either criminal or mentally defective.

Let us use the United States as an example. As is true everywhere, workers have formed labour unions as primary expressions of their growing grasp of the exploitative nature of capitalism. From the beginning, unions were condemned by employers, the media, and the judiciary as, at best, quasi-legal organizations. They were vilified so uniformly that much of the public came to view them as socially illegitimate.

This perception deepened as soon as workers' organizations could be associated with communism and anarchism. The most profound critics of capitalism were also revolutionaries who saw that only the overthrow of capitalism could bring liberation to those oppressed within it. Capitalists saw immediately that such people were the most dangerous to their rule. They began a relentless propaganda campaign against radicals, and they castigated anyone and any organization that had anything in common with them, no matter how tenuous. Unions were communist or anarchist, and by definition un-American, beyond the pale, and deserving of persecution and prosecution. Newspapers portrayed union organizers as unshaven, ape-like, bomb-throwing anarchists. Photographs were doctored to put guns in the hands of "radical" strikers. Provocateurs were placed by police inside unions and other working class groups to urge violence, which could then be laid at the hands of "red" agitators.

Two further developments that intensified the war of ideas were the institution of mandatory public schooling and the promotion of a strong sense of nationalism in every capitalist society. The two were intimately connected, as one of the primary functions of public schooling has been to instill in children a blind devotion to country. The schools, however, have broader purposes. They are authoritarian in their structure, and they teach respect for authority—of employers and the government. Individualism is stressed, and group cohesion and solidarity are condemned. In our public schools, the nation's economic system is glorified as the embodiment of freedom and democracy, and radical ideas, actions, and institutions are decried. Class is ignored or denied.

In some countries, private religious schools are important components of the education system. Such schools differ little from public schools in terms of the values they try to instill in students. The alleged atheism of the socialists, communists, and anarchists is played up more than in public schools, and adds one more negative characteristic to those who champion the cause of workers. In the United States, the Catholic Church played a significant role in getting its members to refuse support for the more radical and militant unions organizing workers during the Great Depression.

While schools serve a critical ideological function, they also are tied to the world of work. They teach certain skills, such as basic literacy and numeracy, that employers need workers to have. The values that the schools teach are also essential to employers; the characteristics the schools honor are the same as those that supervisors reward. Today, schools teach the computer basics required on so many jobs.

Of all the techniques of ideological warfare, the promotion of nationalism is the most important. If workers can be convinced that the essential aspect of their lives is that they are Americans or Canadians or Chinese, then they will not think of themselves primarily as workers and their class consciousness will be buried underneath their patriotism. Besides mandatory public schooling, the key event shaping nationalism is war. War defines foreign workers as national enemies, as "others" deserving to be killed. What could dampen international class consciousness more than this? German and French workers might face the same employers and be much alike, but if Germany and France are at war, the common consciousness that might have developed will instead warp into murder and ethnic hatred.

Once the institutions of ideological warfare are in place and functioning, it becomes possible to invent a new capitalist "reality." Instead of capitalists exploiting workers to generate the profits needed for capital accumulation, we have free markets in which workers and employers meet one another as equals. The market decides what wage will be paid; employers have nothing to do with it. As Adam Smith, one of capitalism's first myth-makers, said, there is an invisible hand that guides the market toward an equilibrium in which workers get what they want (employment and a wage) and employers get what they want (labour to go along with the other means of production). The markets are free, and if workers do not like what a market yields, they can seek employment elsewhere. There is no compulsion.

If workers want high wages, they must make the appropriate individual choices, those that will make their labour more productive and thus deserving of higher wages. According to Smith and his progeny, wage differences among workers are reflections of productivity differences. In the marketplace, each worker and each employer is an isolated individual, free to do as he or she pleases. It is therefore up to the workers to make the right investments in their human capital, so that their labour is productive enough to obtain a high wage. Among the things that enhance productivity are, first and foremost, schooling and training. Workers with small amounts of these will not be productive and will not earn high wages. It might seem irrational for workers to choose such a path, but this is not so. Some workers have an inherent preference for satisfying themselves in the present rather than sacrificing now (getting educated and trained) so that their future wage will be higher. They will naturally, but not unfairly, receive lower wages than their future-oriented brothers and sisters.

It is assumed by the economists that workers supply their labour voluntarily and not out of necessity. To them, work gives pain rather than pleasure and therefore requires a wage to overcome the hurt. What gives pleasure is the consuming of goods and services, and it is necessary for workers to receive a wage to buy these. It is pointless for workers to seek satisfaction from labour; work is innately unsatisfying. No doubt this idea resonates most strongly in Christian countries, where workers are likely to be familiar with the biblical story of Adam and Eve. It also fits nicely with what employers do to control workers. They degrade work with the detailed division of labour to make money. So work cannot be very satisfying in capitalism, but workers won't see this if they believe work is inevitably unsatisfying.

The mythical capitalism of economists tells workers that the impersonal and equal interactions between them and employers in labour markets must not be interfered with by outside forces. The invisible hand must be left to do its perfect work. The two outside forces most worrisome to the economists are the government and labour unions. The government must not, in a push for greater fairness, institute policies such as a minimum wage, national health care, or social security. These will warp the "magic of the marketplace" and end up hurting those they are supposed to help. A minimum wage will lead to more unemployment as some workers are not productive enough to warrant employers paying a higher wage. Unions will do the same thing by forcing employers to pay above-market wages, and leading workers, by giving them greater security, to become less productive, forcing employers to get rid of them.

Once hired, workers are encouraged to believe that they and their employer are in the same boat. Both must cooperate to out-compete other companies and secure the workers' future. All workers in a nation must work hard to make sure that other nations do not gain the upper hand in world markets. The media bombard workers with images of satisfied and happy employees, like the associates in the Wal-Mart commercials.

Ideological warfare, then, consists of the creation of institutions such as public education and national armies and the promulgation of an economic myth. These twin weapons discourage workers from thinking of themselves as an oppressed class that must fight collectively against employers and encourages them to think of anybody but their employers as the causes of their class misery. The government is to blame, unions are to blame, foreigners are to blame, they themselves are to blame.

The fact that workers are objectively exploited by their employers has important and negative consequences for them. They are more likely to suffer poor health than their employers and have lower life expectancies. They are more likely to be injured at work. They will suffer bouts of unemployment, sometimes long ones, and these will cause many difficulties, from a higher likelihood of suicide to a greater chance of being arrested and going to prison. They will be forced to abandon their communities and move themselves and their families to distant places when their workplaces close. They will not be able to save much money, either to fund schooling for their children or to accumulate inheritable wealth. They will suffer all the slings and arrows of employment in capitalism: speed-up and overwork, loss of control over the timing and pace of work and the quality of the product, denial of dignity, and lack of concern for obligations outside the workplace.

However, because of the successful ideological warfare waged by employers, it is difficult for workers to understand what is happening to them. Instead they come to have a false consciousness, one that plays directly into the hands of their bosses.

I do not mean to imply that workers are automatons, programmed to do what the system tells them to do and to believe what it tells them to believe. We can see that this is not true. They have organized labour unions, and through them they have fought their employers and won many things, from higher wages and decent benefits to the right to challenge managerial actions. They have formed political organizations and parties that have compelled governments to enact laws helpful to workers and program which, in some countries, constitute a thoroughgoing welfare state.

Two things must be said, however, with respect to workers as active agents. First, once capitalism has matured, it is unlikely that workers will develop class consciousness autonomously. There are too many forces operating to prevent this.

We see the most radical and unmediated responses to capitalism in less-developed capitalist societies, among both workers and peasants. Such responses are never completely spontaneous. There are always leaders and teachers. But these become more necessary the more developed capitalism becomes.

Second, any organizations workers form to combat their oppression will find it difficult to avoid being influenced by the hegemony capitalism seeks to impose over society. It has been the rule rather than the exception that labour unions become bureaucratic and conservative, even if they were radical in the beginning. The labour movement in the United States, for example, was an active participant in the anti-worker Cold War, purging and persecuting its left-led unions and radical union leaders. Unions in the rich capitalist countries have actively supported the imperialism of their nation's businesses and governments. Unions around the world have been sexist, racist, and homophobic, dividing workers just as surely as have the employers they fight against.

In summary, it is difficult for workers to grasp what happens to them every day in work and respond in a class-conscious way. To the extent that they do become class conscious, they achieve only a partial and tainted consciousness, and this is reflected in the organizations they form. The relentlessness of capitalism can wear down even its purest opponents.

My own life and work illustrate these problems. I was fortunate to have had a job that both allowed the time for and encouraged clear thinking. Yet the structure in which a job is embedded and the varied relationships that a person develops in it and in personal life can still cloud the mind and lead to actions that support the class structure, no matter how radical you think you are.

The position of a college professor in a society's class structure is not always clear. On the one hand, we work for a wage and are therefore members of the working class. But much of what we do supports and strengthens the power of the capitalist class. We confer important class-biased credentials, such as law degrees, and, unwittingly or not, we wage ideological warfare on behalf of society's rulers, both in terms of what we teach and how we teach it. Neoclassical economics is nothing if not the economics of the ruling class. It is important to struggle within the colleges and universities to bring about change, but we shouldn't expect too much. Fighting to make higher education more democratic and responsive to the needs of the working class is akin to doing the same things in our print media. Some good can be done, but only newspapers controlled by the working class can provide the news workers need to know. Similarly, colleges and universities won't help to liberate us until we run them. Furthermore, collective conflict inside academe can't have much impact on the larger society, at least not now and not in most of the world. It would be more important for there to be a radical union of long-distance truck drivers and railroad workers than one of college professors.

When I was a professor, I hoped that by organizing the teachers and the other campus workers, we could help build a different college and, as other teachers did the same, that we could become part of a larger movement that could help transform society. We failed four times to unionize the faculty, and though some professors around the country did form unions, their unions were no different than any others and typically ignored the plight of part-time teachers and those with nontenure stream appointments, two groups that now comprise the majority of instructors on most campuses.

I became a labour educator when I realized that not much was possible inside a college other than influencing a few good students and that it was impossible for me not to sometimes act in the interests of the administration, as when I agreed that a teacher should not be recommended for tenure. As I taught steelworkers, autoworkers, nurses, public school teachers, garment workers, clerical workers, postal employees, and dozens of others, I reconnected with the working class in a more satisfactory way. What I had to say might directly affect a union-organizing campaign, a strike, a worker or union litigating an unfair labour practice, or a contract negotiation. I had to restructure my materials and lectures to fit my new audiences — working men and women coming to class in their free time and without earning academic credits. My presentations had to be more immediate and engaging or people would get up and leave. My experiences over many years acquainted me with workers throughout western Pennsylvania and then across the country. They also encouraged me and gave me a language to write articles and books for, rather than about, the working class.

But if I taught workers at night and on weekends, I still had to labour at the college. Compounding the frustration I felt knowing how infertile academe's grounds were for the growth of a radical social movement were two depressing developments. First, in the 1980s my college, like most others, succumbed more or less completely to the marketplace. The central university began to more brazenly use our campus as a source of revenue to fund its larger purposes — to pay for research facilities and staff to investigate social and scientific problems intimately tied to the needs of corporations and national defence. To obtain the largest surplus possible, we were forced to accept an ever-growing student body with a relatively smaller teaching staff. Class sizes and number of course preparations mushroomed while compensation stagnated. Those majors that might help students think critically were starved of funds and teachers, while those that better fit our students for low-level managerial and technical employment were either put in place or expanded. More resources were devoted to measuring our performance — evaluations of all sorts — than to building faculty teaching and research capacities.

Second, our students were of a different character than those I had taught in the beginning. The local economy collapsed as the northern steel industry was shredded by high interest rates, international competition, corporate downsizing, outsourcing, and geographical relocation. The enthusiastic first-generation college students we once taught disappeared with the mills. We replaced them with mediocre and uninterested youngsters from the middle-class suburbs of Pittsburgh. These students were not my cup of tea. They saw college as a place to party and a way station in between high school and the real world. They expected to get a degree, and the better job and money that went with it, simply because they had purchased their place in our classrooms. If they didn't do well with minimum effort, it wasn't their fault. The product (the education they had purchased, of which I was an integral part, like the power cord on a computer) must be defective. They resented learning and made their disdain obvious.

These twin evils made it hard to imagine many more years of them. I disliked my job so much that I entered therapy. My therapist suggested that I find a way to quit and then retire with dignity. Simple but profound. Our children were adults, and my pension was growing rapidly. My wife and I calculated that it would be possible to leave my job at fifty-five, the age at which I could withdraw money from the pension without tax penalty. We wouldn't be rich, but we could live without full-time employment. We could take part-time jobs if we needed more money. I decided to do this, and once I did, the relief was palpable. I could stop participating in an academic shell game, and I wouldn't have to face those blank stares again. I taught my last class at the college in April 2001. Fittingly, it was a seminar on Marx's *Capital*.

Leaving a job I had for thirty-two years was not difficult. What was hard was figuring out what to do with the rest of my life. I had been as true to the working class as I could be in my classrooms and in the college. I had gone beyond being a radical academic, tilting so often at windmills and being part of a conservative and ideologically repressive institution no matter what I did, and directly engaged the working class as a labour educator. It might have been natural then for me to work for a union or some other working class organization. Or perhaps I could become a full-time labour educator. Neither of these appealed to me. As my story of the United Farm Workers shows, it is not easy and often impossible to be a radical inside a union, maybe more so than in a university. Even the best unions burn out their staffs, and few devote sufficient time to member education. What education unions do do is devoid of radical content. Unions are as fearful of "reds" as are the businesses they meet at the bargaining table. Politically and ideologically, the U.S. labour movement is moribund, long on providing funds for Democratic politicians and short on a radical imagination.

There are no independent labour education programs in the country, at least not ones that pay for the work done. Worker education is either done within unions, with the attendant problems just discussed, or it is housed in a university. To teach full-time in one of these would be going from the frying pan into the fire. I didn't leave one college to go to another one. College-based labour education programs usually have two parts: a typical liberal arts major or certificate and classes and training done in conjunction with specific unions or groups of workers. The latter outreach component is the critical one, since it directly connects the educators to the working class. The unions have some control over this because their funding is important for the survival of the department and staff, but there is a chance that the curriculum can be more independent and radical than union-centred education. It is this kind of teaching that I had done for many years. However, universities, sometimes in alignment with faculty, have been gutting outreach efforts and instead devoting resources to the academic part of labour education. The result is just another college department, no different than any other and unlikely to generate radical thought and action in the labour movement.

A working life is difficult and takes a heavy toll on mind and body. If the transformation of the system cannot realistically be imagined in a lifetime, it is natural to want to escape it. Wage labour is wage labour no matter the employer. I thought that I could teach if I needed or wanted to, and I could write whenever I felt like it. My wife and I decided to radically change our lives after I quit teaching. We gave away nearly all our possessions—to our four children, to libraries, to friends, to charities, to people who needed these things more than we did. What was left we packed in our Plymouth van and hit the road. For the past seven years, we have roamed the United States, living in Yellowstone National Park (where I worked as a hotel desk clerk), Manhattan (where I helped edit a left-wing magazine), in Portland, Oregon (where I began to teach workers in internet classes), in Miami Beach, Estes Park, Colorado, Tucson, and Amherst, Massachusetts. We have gone on long road trips—of 120, 150, 157, and 105 days—seeing the country up close and personal. I have been writing and speaking about our travels, trying to tell people the truths about being a worker in a capitalist society. I don't know whether I am in the working class or not. But I've still got my shoulder to the wheel of the struggle for a society where there are no classes at all.

A Lucky Man

FICTION

Sometimes a random event can change a person's life. Clyde Yassem was sitting in the fire hall drinking stale coffee and sneaking a look at *The Daily Racing Form* when the emergency phone rang. He answered it, thinking that this would be his first crisis call.

"Fireman Yassem here," Clyde said.

A woman's voice said, "A pallet of glass fell on a guy down here in packing. He's hurt bad. Get here quick. Park the truck by the first aid room."

Clyde recognized the woman, one of the nurses. Her sister was a nurse too, at the hospital. While he was waiting for his first kid to be born, she brought out a black baby and told Clyde it was his son. Thought it was a great joke.

Clyde ran down the steps and jumped in his truck. He hit the siren, drove down the road in front of the fire hall, and entered the plant at an opening a few yards from the river. He snaked his way though the dimly lit corridors and stopped near a large overhead crane, beneath which was a large pile of shattered plate glass and where a large group of workers surrounded a man slumped on the floor. Clyde ordered someone to help him with a stretcher. The nurse was cleaning wounds on the man's head and arms. He was unconscious and his body was contorted into a grotesque position that reminded Clyde right away of wounded men he had seen in the war. The nurse said she had called the local hospital and that they would be waiting outside the emergency room for Clyde's truck. Clyde and several of the men lifted the man as carefully as they could onto the stretcher, tied him in, and hoisted him into the back of the ambulance. One of them agreed to go along and stay in the back with the injured worker. Clyde started the engine and raced out of the plant and to the hospital as fast as he could. He was nervous and gingerly hit the siren and pressed his foot down hard on the gas pedal.

The hospital was three miles away. Clyde only remembered the noise of the siren and the lights of the swerving oncoming traffic as he changed lanes to keep up his speed. As he sailed through a traffic light, he suddenly remembered who the man on the stretcher was. A friend of his, Ed Smolen, one of the boys he'd enlisted with in 1941. He delivered Ed to the emergency entrance, signed some forms, and hung around the waiting room for a while. Ed's wife arrived, and Clyde tried to comfort her. She kept saying. "What are we going to do if Ed can't work." A doctor came out and told him that they were performing surgery. They wouldn't know for a few days if Ed would recover. Clyde might as well go back to the factory.

Clyde Yassem was a factory worker. He had been one for twenty-two years. He hadn't planned it. At night sometimes, he lay awake next to his wife and wondered how it had happened. As a boy he hadn't had much ambition. During the Great Depression, it didn't seem to make much sense to be ambitious. Nearly everyone in town was unemployed or working short hours. Parents found it hard to give their children encouragement about the future; they had little enough hope for it themselves. So, like his friends, he drifted through high school, barely passing most of his classes and skipping school at least once a week to shoot pool, go swimming in the river, or loaf at the drugstore. The teachers seemed to accept their students' indifference. They hadn't been paid regularly, and many of them had been laid off, too. The kids thought it was quite a joke when the truant officer was put on furlough. The teachers didn't know what to do with their charges, so they let them do what they wanted. As did their parents. Clyde's mom and dad did put him in a Civilian Conservation Corps camp in 1938. He hadn't minded this, even though it involved hard work and army-like discipline. At least it was something to do.

Clyde's friends were gung-ho for sports. His dad was a good athlete and still played semi-pro baseball in the summers. Clyde liked sports, too, but he wasn't good at them. He had been a sickly child and had spent nearly two years in a sanitarium for tuberculosis when he was two years old. He was fine now, but he didn't have much strength and stamina. It was a sore point with him, especially when someone brought up his father's athletic prowess. To make matters worse, he was skinny, and this made him the butt of jokes, even among his pals. In the rough-and-tumble world of the children of factory workers, physical vigour was a virtue above all others. He still remembered with shame the times he had backed down from fights or was the last chosen in pick-up games of baseball. Some big Polish kid, his head shaved for the summer, would say, "I guess we're stuck with you, Clyde."

Somehow he managed to graduate high school, probably because everyone who lasted twelve years did. A kind of consolation prize for perseverance in the face of bleak future prospects. The following week, Clyde applied for a job at the factory, as did nearly all of his classmates. It was 1940, and the looming war in Europe had put more men to work. For the first time in years, new employees were being hired. Clyde was among them, undoubtedly because his father worked there. He remembered the first day, how nervous he was as he walked through the long tunnel under the railroad tracks into the plant. He reported to a foreman amidst the noise, dust, and disarray. The foreman said, "Don't give me no shit, kid, and you'll be OK." He was set to work packing glass into crates. It was boring, hard work, but this was where everyone started. He hoped that he might be able to get into one of the apprentice programs and learn a craft, maybe plumbing or electric, something he might use outside the plant someday.

Clyde slogged on for a year and a half. He worked steadily, though not always full-time. He was still packing glass, but his dad was trying to get him an apprenticeship, so things might get better. He had a steady girlfriend, a pretty Italian kid from the mining town down the river. On weekends, he'd walk the six miles to her house. She lived with her mother and brother in a small mining company shack. He couldn't believe how poor they were. No bathroom, not even hot water. The mother took in laundry and cleaned the local doctor's house. At one point they had all taken a job unloading dynamite at the coalmine along the river. Miners used the explosive to open new seams of coal. All three of them would walk down the steep hill to the mine and unload the heavy boxes. After they finished, they stumbled home in the throes of asthma attacks and collapsed on the couch until breath returned. His girlfriend eventually got a job cleaning the mine company offices on Saturday and once had to fend off the advances of the superintendent. The mining village might be just six miles from the factory town, but it was another world.

Like everyone else, Clyde Yassem remembered what he had been doing on December 7, 1941. Sleeping. His parents and two of his younger brothers rushed in to awaken him and tell him the news. He didn't think much of it at first, but as what happened became clear, he could see that it had electrified the town. People talked of little else, and within a few days, young men were driving, taking the train, or hitchhiking to the next town up the river to the military recruiting offices. A patriotic fever swept the nation, and everyone was now paying attention to events in Europe and Asia. There were no Japanese-Americans in Clyde's town, but the many families of German ancestry found themselves suspect by their neighbors. Some teenagers had vandalized the German Beneficial Union club after a report in the big city paper said that the GBU was a hotbed of homegrown Nazis.

So many young factory workers were enlisting that the management began to keep workers on the job for ten and sometimes twelve hours a day, something it hadn't done since 1929. Thanks to the new federal law, hours over forty a week had to be paid at time and one-half the regular hourly wage rate, and this meant that the men, including Clyde, were bringing home record paychecks. But Clyde was as caught up in war fever as anyone else. He had a good number and might not have been called up in the draft the government had initiated. But he wanted to join up and fight the Japs. So, in May 1942 he visited the naval recruiting office. A friend had told him that you had a better chance to survive in the navy than in the army or marines. He just made the weight minimum, and when the doctor asked him about the red marks on his knuckles, which were scars left from the tuberculosis that had attacked his bones as a child, he told the doctor that he had fallen. Remarkably, the physician didn't probe further.

Before he left for basic training, Clyde Yassem married his girlfriend, much to the chagrin of his parents, who were none too keen on Italian-Americans. This didn't matter to him; he was in love and already planning to have a large family when he got back from the war. His wife would stay with her mother, and his parents would look after the cheap car he had bought a few months before.

The war and his marriage seemed to change everything for Clyde. It sounds silly to say it but it was true—the war made him a man. It took him out of his small, provincial town, mixed him with guys from all over the country, put him in the best physical shape of his life (even if he did have to be pushed off a rock to get him to swim), sent him far away to the South Pacific, showed him that he could face physical danger, made him a lifelong friend of the Samoan people, and taught him a skill. This last he had learned in temporary classrooms at the University of Chicago, where he was sent to radio school. Here he learned to take down and transmit code, to operate short wave radios, and to string wire in battle zones. Not many of his classmates made it through the school; for the first time in his life he stood out as someone who could do something not everyone else could do. It was stressful work, but he could do it calmly and without making mistakes. By the time he shipped out, he could light a cigarette while taking code and remember what had been transmitted while he was doing this.

Having a wife gave him a sense of security hard to put into words. It was evidence that he was a person someone else could love. He longed for the responsibility of a family, and from wherever he was, he cut pictures of children from magazines and sent them home. He also devised a way to trick the censors and tell his wife where he was when he got to the war zones. He told her that he would send a letter as soon as he could and that the second letter of the first word in every sentence would give her his location. She'd have to look it up on a good map. He was first stationed on the island of Funafuti in the Ellice Islands.

Clyde's actual wartime service was relatively uneventful. He saw some awful things and a couple of close buddies were killed, but in the main, he did what he did and saw what he saw and, luckily, nothing bad happened to him and he didn't come out of the war either physically or psychologically wrecked. One amazing thing happened one night while he was listening to Tokyo Rose. She sometimes "interviewed" prisoners of war, and on this night he heard the voice of a fellow from his hometown. His wife had sent him a clipping from the local paper reporting that this man was missing in action and presumed dead, a reasonable assumption since the Japanese didn't take many prisoners and often killed the ones they did capture. After he heard his hometown boy, he wrote his wife who, when she finally got the letter, told the family. Their son was alive, and their lives were restored.

Like most of the soldiers in the South Pacific, Clyde came home a few months after the bombs fell on Hiroshima and Nagasaki. First he was sent to East Texas where he was joined by his wife. She became pregnant not long after, but before their first child was born they were back in his hometown and he was again working in the factory. His hopes were high. A big strike was called not long after he started, and it was a great victory for the workers, who stood firm and solidly together, something many of them had learned to do in the war. You could count on your buddies and no one else. Together, you had a chance to get what you wanted, whether it was survival in the war or a fatter paycheck and benefits back in the civilian world. Clyde figured he would save some money and start a small business. He was envisioning a radio repair shop and had bought a used Hallicrafters short wave radio to practise on. He was also thinking about taking a correspondence course in drafting or something like that. Post-war America was an optimistic place, and Clyde had absorbed some of the good feelings all around him.

"Hey, Clyde, how's it going."

"Not too bad, Hap. My wife says I'm starting to look like a bum. I guess it's time for a haircut."

"Chair's empty," said Hap.

Hap Fidzik owned a combination barbershop and poolroom. He did all right raking his cut from the tables when the good players were hustling, but the real money came from selling numbers. He did a brisk business. Working men loved to gamble. Clyde did. He won a lot of money playing poker in the navy. Men stuck on an island with time to kill were easy marks for a man who didn't drink. He sometimes shot craps at lunchtime in the factory or caught a little action after work at a local club where there was always a game. When he had a dream about a number, he played it at Hap's. Gambling got the adrenaline flowing, and he was a keen observer of the little ticks and gestures that played over guys' faces when money was on the line. Win, and even the cheapskates got generous. Lose, and most lost their composure. Clyde liked it when other players said he was lucky. Maybe he was, but he played smart, watched his money, never lost the mortgage payment.

What Clyde enjoyed most were the horses. There were two racetracks an hour's drive from town. One was for thoroughbreds, the other for pacers and trotters. He tried to get to a track once a week, usually on Saturdays, but with a family, he couldn't always go, so he often booked bets at Hap's. His approach was systematic. He kept a notebook with records from the newspapers of recent winners and near winners. He watched for hot jockeys and drivers. He noticed which horses were good in bad weather. Whenever he could, he got a copy of the *Daily Racing Form* in a nearby town and read and reread every issue. His work was rewarded; he won consistently—not much, since he didn't have much to bet, but enough to help pay the bills and allow for small luxuries like a take-out pizza or a trip to the drive-in hamburger stand.

For all but a few of us, optimism is hard to sustain without a surplus of money. Even union wages don't allow for savings if a person wants to live a normal life. Clyde and his wife had a second child and then a third. To house their family, they decided to take on one of the new mortgages being guaranteed by the government and aimed at veterans like Clyde. They had a small house built on the hill overlooking the town. They couldn't afford the plan with a fireplace, but still they got a nice house with a big yard, just right for raising kids. He planted a garden, and his wife canned beans, tomatoes, and peaches. Kids and a mortgage took up most of his paycheck, and it wasn't long before Clyde tried to get as much overtime as he could. After ten years of factory work, he seldom thought of his old dreams of radio repair and drafting. He was a glass-worker. There were worse things he could be doing. Like dreaming about things that weren't going to happen.

"Clyde, you see these new football sheets?"

"What?"

"The football pool sheets. Every week, I get a bunch of them. College and pro games are listed with the point spreads. You can bet on one game, two games, or as many as you like. If you bet on more than one, all your teams have to beat the spot for you to win. The odds get higher the more teams you pick."

"Sounds like a good deal for you," Clyde said. "The suckers will see the big payoff and not the sucker's bets."

"Yeah," Hap said, "all you dreamers will make me rich." Clyde could have been a wise guy and told Hap that he'd already contributed to more than one divorce, but he was thinking that here might be an opportunity to stretch his paycheck.

"Hey, Hap, I bet I could sell a lot of those sheets in the plant. I just bid on a job in the fire department. I passed all the tests and, with my seniority, I'm a lock for the job. A fireman makes safety checks in the plant every day, so I'll be in every department in the factory. You get more time to do the safety inspections than it really takes, so I'll have time to talk to the guys and sell them football sheets. Everybody's an expert on football; they'll eat these things up."

"Clyde, I like that idea. Let me know when you get the job and I'll set you up with the sheets."

Within a month of starting his new job, Clyde was selling more than 100 pool sheets a week and earning at least an extra $50. Big money in those days. Even the foremen were buying them. Hap always paid the winners on Monday, and the site of happy men counting their money was the best advertising Clyde could get. By the end of the first season, Clyde was dreaming of a new car.

A factory is a battle zone. Nothing better illustrates the slogan that "time is money" than the daily struggle between workers and bosses to squeeze a little more free time or a little more work out of the workday. The time-study guy would sneak around with his stopwatch, ever on the lookout for a motion to be saved so that another fraction of a second of work could be added to the daily grind. The men watched for him and devised ingenious ways to pretend to be working. If you could start working at 8:02 instead of 8:00, take an extra three minutes for lunch, or line up in front of the time clock a few minutes before the shift ended, you'd beaten the system. Same thing if you lingered in the toilet stall reading the newspaper. A minor injury that sent you home early with a full day's pay was a sublime victory. If the boss had you do something forbidden by the contract, you licked your lips in anticipation of the grievance you'd file and the backpay you might win. Some guys had learned how to do two jobs along the assembly line, theirs and their buddies', and each would relieve the other for as long as half a shift. This worked especially well when the foreman was in a meeting.

As Clyde wandered around the plant inspecting the safety stations and selling football sheets, he watched the wars play out in each department and listened to the men bitch about the company, and often enough, each other.

"Hey, Clyde, your old man comes down here again with that stopwatch and I'm going to smack him."

"Hey, Clyde, how come you're the only white motherfucker comes down here? Only us niggers in the foundry. Man, the Steelers are a lock this week. Same for the Browns. Give me some sheets."

"Clyde, those niggers'll be up here soon. Mark my words."

"Clyde, tell those union guys to stop sipping free coffee in the fire hall and get down here and tell this fucking foreman he better check those machines. Someone's going to get hurt soon."

"Clyde, they're screwing up my incentive pay every week."

"Clyde, these sonsabitches want me to OK bad glass. Fuck 'em, I won't do it."

"Clyde, we're going to walk out they keep speeding up the line."

Back at the fire hall, the firemen sat around drinking coffee and gossiping when they weren't doing daily chores or called to some emergency. Clyde heard the local union officers who came by every day for the free joe do the same. Clyde and his buddies told them the things they'd heard, and between the firemen and the union chiefs, there wasn't much that went on in the factory that went unnoticed. The plant manager always seemed surprised that the union knew things it wasn't supposed to know.

Like most of the men, he went to the union when he had a problem. Some guys were interested in running the union; this was what they did, like he played the ponies and sold football sheets. He knew little of the sit-down strikes that had spawned the CIO and nothing of the wobblies and Joe Hill. He read in the papers about all the communists in some unions, and he'd heard his dad badmouth the unions often enough. He neither loved nor hated the company. He was mad when his father had time-studied him but mainly because it seemed like a betrayal; his old man's loyalty to the company trumped his loyalty to his son.

One thing kept bothering Clyde, though. He couldn't get the look on Ed Smolen's wife's face after the accident out of his mind. On the return drive from the hospital that day, Clyde had recalled a conversation in the fire hall with the union vice-president. The union safety committee had warned the company more than once about that crane. The foreman had promised to have it inspected and overhauled but never did. Now Ed's body was mangled. "Jesus lover!" Clyde had said to himself.

Ed Smolen didn't die, but he never walked again. He got workers' compensation, and his family got a harder life. When Clyde kept talking about Ed and the accident, one of the firemen said, "If you're so concerned about what happened to Ed, why don't you start going to union meetings and do something about it." A couple of months later, Clyde did. As he listened to the committee reports, his head got heavy and he started to daydream. Maybe this was a waste of time. Then, after the safety committee chairman spoke, a man in the back of the room shouted, "What about that crane that crippled Ed Smolen?"

"We're on that," said the union president.

"Not fast enough. It's still not been inspected. Somebody else got to get hurt before we do something?"

The meeting erupted into a shouting match, with Ed's workmates yelling at the union brass and the union president trying as best he could to defend himself. In the end, the workers agreed that a delegation from Ed's department would go unannounced the next day to the plant manager's office and demand some action. Clyde hung around after the meeting talking to the guys about the trip to the hospital and how afraid Ed's wife had been. He even sold a couple of football sheets. To everyone's surprise, the crane inspector showed up at the start of the 8:00 a.m. shift, before the men gathered to confront the plant manager. They went anyway.

Clyde seldom missed a union meeting after that. Within a year, he was like a convert to a new religion—more committed and fanatic than those who had been faithful all their lives. Everything was seen in a new light, and the embers of his class awakening became a fire. He started to argue with his father. When his dad said over dinner that Ed probably wasn't following proper safety procedures when he was hurt, Clyde swore and left the table. Clyde still sold his betting sheets, but now he came with a message. Don't trust the company. Support the union.

Clyde volunteered for the union safety committee, and a year later he was elected its chairman. A year later, he was elected chief union steward. After the president, this was the most important union office. A steward was the union's first line of defence in the plant: the man who brought new workers into the union; informed workers of their rights under the con-tract; submitted, investigated, and fought grievances. As head steward, Clyde could go anywhere in the plant at any time to perform his duties.

Some stewards waited for members to come to them with complaints; then they would investigate them, try to settle matters amicably with the foreman, and file a grievance as a last resort. Clyde was aggressive. He met regularly with men and women in all departments, looking for problems and encour-aging grievances, the more the better. He wasn't above threat-ening a foreman with a work slowdown or four flat tires to get a problem resolved. The grievance procedure was structured as series of steps: informal meeting with a foreman; formal grievance and meeting with the department head; meeting of the plant-wide grievance committee with the plant manager's staff; and, if these failed, arbitration, in which a neutral third party, selected by company and union, decided whether the grievance had merit or not and assessed the penalty against the employer if it did. Clyde loved the sit-downs with the plant manager's labour relations staff. He was always better prepared than they, and he relished showing off his knowledge to the other stewards and union officers. They'd go back and tell the men how he'd put it to the company. Clyde also led the union in arbitrations. He learned how to prepare witness-es and examine them. The union's attorney said he'd never seen anyone better. When Clyde pushed a grievance through arbitration, the union usually won. People began to say that Clyde would make a good union president when the old incumbent retired. Clyde didn't discourage such talk.

The bosses don't like a good union man. They can deal with the ambitious bureaucrats, the compromisers, the glad-handlers. But the guy who goes for the jugular every time, who sees each grievance as a struggle of good against evil, well, that's another matter. Out of deference to Clyde's father, the company tread softly at first. They asked his father to talk to him. When this failed, they suggested to his dad that Clyde might make a good supervisor. Clyde told his father that he couldn't be bought. The men had rights under the contract, and he intended to see that they were upheld. He reminded his father that about half of the grievances were for company safety violations. Maybe if the company was as concerned about safety as it was about bribing him, he wouldn't have to file so many grievances in the first place. And maybe if the company cared about men not getting maimed and cut, Ed Smolen would still be walking. Clyde's dad lit a cigar and said, "Clyde, it might not be a good idea to get so radical."

A few weeks after his father's talk, the fire chief called him into his office. Clyde thought maybe they were going to discuss some complaints the firemen had made about overtime and shift changes. But when he saw the head of labour relations seated in the big leather chair next to the chief's desk, he knew something was up. The chief told him to sit down. He did, and the labour relations guy, Art Bowser, started to talk to him. He sounded like he was reading from a script. "Clyde," he said, "I'm sure you're familiar with Article Nineteen of the contract."

Clyde said, "Yes, that deals with discipline and discharge."

"Right," said Art, "We have a situation with someone committing an illegal act while on company premises and during work time."

Clyde thought, shit, some asshole came to work drunk. The agreement said that anyone obviously inebriated could be summarily discharged. Clyde had dealt with three drinking discharges so far, and each time the company had agreed to lessen the penalty to a three-day suspension. None of the cases had gone to arbitration. Clyde said, "Did someone come to work drunk again?"

"No," said Art, "This time someone has been running a gambling racket." Art looked at Clyde and said, "You've been selling football pool sheets, collecting money, and making payouts for months, haven't you Clyde?"

Clyde saw what was coming. Payback for filing all those grievances. But he smiled and said, "Sure, quite a few of your guys buy tickets every week."

Art said, "We've already fired six foremen, just today, for illegal gambling. When we find out who else has been involved, we'll fire them, too."

Clyde said, "I want a union rep present. Now."

"Sure," said Art. He motioned to the chief to bring in the grievance man from the fire department. The chief made a call and in a few minutes the rep arrived. An hour later, Clyde was escorted through the gate and onto the street by a company security guard.

Clyde's wife cried when he told her what happened. "I told you not to get involved in that stuff with the union. Now what are we going to do?" Clyde said, "Fuck the company. We'll win this grievance just like we've won all the others. I'll get back to work and a big chunk of back pay, too."

The union filed a grievance on Clyde's behalf the same day he was fired. At the union hall the next day, Clyde urged direct action by the men. Wildcat strikes, work slowdowns, pickets at the gates. If the company could fire the head of the grievance committee for doing something as petty as selling football sheets and get away with it, what was next? The officers agreed and told Clyde to go home and start preparing his defence.

Clyde expected action right away, but a week later nothing had happened. He started making phone calls to men from all the departments in the plant, asking what was going on. They said that the men were ready to hit the bricks, picket, whatever it took to get Clyde back. But the union president and vice-president were urging caution. One of Clyde's buddies told him that he smelled a rat. At a nearby bar a couple of weeks ago, he'd overheard the union vice-president tell a guy who didn't like Clyde that maybe Clyde was too radical to be union president. Maybe the powers that be in the union were not so unhappy that Clyde had been fired. Clyde almost started to cry after he hung up. He hadn't figured on the union being fucked up, too.

As the days passed, Clyde tried to stay optimistic. He met with the union lawyer and planned strategy for the arbitration. When a worker was summarily fired, the first steps of the grievance procedure were skipped, and if the union demanded it, the case went straight to arbitration. They worked out a witness list to show that gambling pools had been routinely administered for more than thirty years, and no one, worker or supervisor, had ever been disciplined for doing so. They developed their main argument, that the reason for Clyde's firing was not his gambling pool but his union activity, his aggressive grievance filing, and success in prosecuting them. Clyde was certain he would win the arbitration. Still, the union's apparent unwillingness to do more made Clyde's spirits sink. He might get his job back, but there would be no triumphant return, no arousal of the men that might make the union stronger.

By the time Clyde got the letter telling him the date of the arbitration hearing, he was nearly out of money. He'd made house payments, but the rest of the bills were overdue and food was in short supply. His parents offered to lend him money, but he refused to borrow from a man who'd never object to what the company had done. He had made a little money betting on the horses. He had plenty of time to study the *Daily Racing Form*.

The old guy who owned the newsstand that sold the form had been a union organizer in the thirties, and when Clyde told him what had happened, he let Clyde have the *Form* on the house. He started making elaborate calculations and charts, picking winners and checking his choices against the results the next day. He placed imaginary bets, and kept track of his winnings. They were substantial. Too bad he didn't have money to bet.

He was downtown drinking coffee at Dot's Diner, reading the sports section of the local paper. "Hey, Clyde. How you doin'?"

Clyde looked up to see his buddy Nick. Clyde said, "Not too bad."

Nick said, "You don't look too good." Clyde filled him in on what had been happening. Nick said he'd heard about most of this. "What a fuckin' shame, you deserve better." Then Nick took an envelope from his pocket and handed it to Clyde. "Don't say nothing. Just take it. It's from some of your buddies." Clyde started to protest, but Nick cut him short. "Just take it."

"See you around," he said. "Keep smiling."

Clyde opened the envelope and counted out $300. Enough to square away his bills. He left the restaurant and started to walk home, thinking how happy his wife would be. A conversation started in his mind.

"I know I could turn some of this money into a lot more at the track."

"No, better not. Might lose it all. Give it to the wife and pay the bills."

"Shit, take $100 to the track. What harm could that do?"

When he got home, Clyde gave his wife $200 and told her what had happened. Like he thought, she was happy. The next day he told her he had to go into the city the following day to meet with some union bigwigs about his case. He said he'd probably be home later in the evening. "They'll feed me something, so don't worry about me for supper."

He left the house at nine o'clock. It was a two-hour drive to the track, and the races started at one o'clock. He'd get there early and study the *Form*. He'd have time to go to the paddock and look at the horses too. He kept feeling in his pocket to make sure the money was there. His heart was racing when he pulled into the parking lot, paid the admission, and bought the *Form*. He pulled his track records from inside his jacket, bought a cup of coffee, and found a place to sit and plan his picks.

When he bought his entrance ticket, he got a program. He started to leaf through it. On the inside cover page, he noticed a promotion the track was running that day. The admission ticket had the same number at each end. Patrons were to rip their tickets in two and place half the ticket inside a steel drum near the track entrance. Ten tickets would be drawn before the first race, which had ten horses scheduled to run. The holders of these tickets would then bring their halves down to the starting gate for verification. Ten tickets with numbers from one to ten printed on them would be drawn from another drum, one ticket drawn by each of the ten winners. The number on the ticket you drew would identify a horse in the first race, number one would be the horse in the number one gate, number two would be the horse in the second gate, and so forth. Whatever a particular horse won in the race would also be won by the holder of the ticket with that horse's number. So if you were one of the lucky ten initial winners and you drew the ticket with the number three stamped on it, you would win whatever the number three horse won that day. In this race, the winnings distribution was

First place horse: $1,000
Second place horse: $600
Third place horse: $200
Fourth place horse: $75
Fifth place horse: $25

Five people would win money. The chance of winning anything was small, but Clyde figured that there was no risk in putting half his ticket in the drum. So he did and went back to the *Form*. He was engrossed in his calculations and jumped when he heard the track announcer's voice telling everyone to turn their attention to the starting gate. It was forty minutes before post time, and the contest drawing was about to begin. Clyde grabbed his ticket from his shirt pocket and waited for the drawing. He memorized his ticket number and when the ninth ticket was drawn, he heard the first three numbers on his ticket. He had a premonition that the next two would match as well, and when they did, he shouted, "Yes." He ran down to the gate and showed the track official his stub. He exchanged congratulations with the other winners and waited for the next drawing. He was the ninth person to pick. He reached into the drum and quickly took one of the two remaining tickets. Number nine. The ten men were admonished to hang on to their stubs and the numbered ticket. The winners were to bring them to the track office right after the race.

Clyde hadn't planned to bet the first race, so he didn't know the horses running. His hopes sank when he looked at the *Form*. The horse's name was Bud Bratty, a four-year-old gelding that had never won a race. A maiden running on the outside in a six furlong sprint. What could be worse? Only that Bud Bratty had never even finished in the money and had lost its last five races by at least fifteen lengths. At the end of the *Form* record of each race a horse had run, there was a line with a brief summary comment. Three of them said, "Trailed far behind." One said, "No factor." Another said, "Stumbled at gate." Clyde's trained eye did notice that in the last race, a distance run of a mile and a quarter, the horse had started well and had led at the half-mile mark. The track condition was listed as "muddy," and maybe that was a good omen, since it had begun to rain about an hour before. But a nag coming out of the nine hole would have to burn a lot of energy getting to the front of the pack. Bud Bratty wouldn't have anything left after that.

Clyde was standing by a betting window, three minutes before race time. He wasn't superstitious, but he thought it was weird that he was the ninth person called, the ninth to pick, and his horse was number nine. When he heard the announcer yell out that it was one minute to post time, he rushed to the window and said, "A hundred dollars on number nine to win." He had never made this large a bet in his life. If he lost, he'd have to go home broke. He ran down to the fence by the finish line and looked at the tote board. Bud Bratty was forty-to-one. He watched the horse enter the starting gate. His horse looked okay; it was calm and had clear eyes. His jockey was talking softly to him. The jockey's name was Santiago. A decent rider, he'd been on Bud Bratty that last trip in the slop. Some late money drove the odds down to thirty-to-one. Clyde thought, "Maybe something's up."

In the movies, the long shot comes from far behind, like Seabiscuit used to do when Clyde was in high school. The gambler would scream in joy and hug his girlfriend. Damon Runyon stuff. But Bud Bratty raced to the front and stayed there. Wire to wire, won by three lengths. Clyde started to smile and couldn't stop. He had won $4,000. Half-a-year's pay. First he went to a cashier's window and watched him count out and hand over thirty one-hundred-dollar bills. Clyde put them safely in the inside zippered pocket of his jacket, watching that no one saw him do this. Then he went to the track's main office and got a check for $1,000. The man who gave him the money said, "You probably never thought that horse would win. You're a lucky man."

Clyde stayed for three more races, but he didn't feel like betting. He was nervous about the money. He looked over the card for the fifth race and decided to go home. Outside the turnstile, on his way to the parking lot, he saw a bunch of discarded tickets. He picked them up and riffled through them.

He saw a nine and looked at that ticket. It was a $10 win bet on Bud Bratty. Some fool had thrown it away. He went back inside and collected another $300.

He was laughing so hard that he nearly ran into a truck as he pulled out of the parking lot and onto the highway. Money! He could live for months on this. Time enough to win his arbitration. Get back to work. Start a caucus in the union and, soon enough, get elected president. Sell football pool sheets out of the union office. Give half the money to the strike fund. A new life from a day at the track. Maybe he was a lucky man.

ACKNOWLEDGMENTS

The good people at Arbeiter Ring showed remarkable patience waiting for me to finish these essays and great skill in making a coherent whole out of them. Special thanks to Esyllt Jones for her encouragement and for suggesting how the original manuscript could be changed and rearranged to make a better book. I appreciated as well the excellent copyediting of Richard Wood. Thanks to the editors at Counterpunch for posting versions of the following essays on their website <www.counterpunch.org>: "At the Wall," "Minstrel Show," and "Taking the Pledge." Thanks to St. Martin's Press for allowing us to use the essay "Teaching the Workers," an earlier version of which appeared in Patricia Meyer Spacks, editor, *Advocacy in the Classroom: Propaganda versus Engagement* (New York: St. Martins Press, 1996). Thanks to *Monthly Review* magazine for permitting us to use the essay "Class: a Personal Story," an earlier version of which appeared in the July/August 2006 issue. "At the Factory Gate" was published many years ago in a now defunct newspaper called *The Mill Hunk Journal*. While no permission is needed to use this, I thank the editors of that journal for allowing my first effort at creative writing to see the light of day.

MICHAEL D. YATES is a writer, editor, and educator. Among his books are *Cheap Motels and a Hotplate: an Economist's Travelogue* (Monthly Review Press, 2007), *Naming the System: Inequality and Work in the Global Economy* (Monthly Review Press, 2002), *Why Unions Matter* (Monthly Review Press, 1998), *Longer Hours, Fewer Jobs* (Monthly Review Press, 1994), and *Power on the Job* (South End Press, 1994). He has also published more than 150 articles and reviews in a wide variety of journals, magazines, and newspapers. His works have been translated into seventeen languages. He is currently Associate Editor of *Monthly Review* magazine. He taught economics and labor relations at the University of Pittsburgh at Johnstown from 1969 until his retirement in 2001. He won the Chancellor's Distinguished Teaching Award in 1984. He currently teaches courses for workers at the University of Indiana, Cornell University, and the University of Massachusetts at Amherst. Yates also worked in the Research Office of the United Farm Workers Union and has served as a labor arbitrator with the Pennsylvania Bureau of Mediation. Yates grew up in Ford City, Pennsylvania. He is married to Karen Korenoski of Dunlo, Pennsylvania. They have four adult children.